IVORY TOWERS
AND DRESSED STONES

The Dovecot, Rivington Terraced Gardens

IVORY TOWERS AND DRESSED STONES

Exploring the Follies, Prospect Towers &
other Curiosities of Northern England
Vol 1: Lancashire

by Jim Jarratt

CICERONE PRESS,
MILNTHORPE, CUMBRIA

© Jim Jarratt 1994
ISBN 1 85284 146 X
A catalogue record for this book is available from the British Library

ACKNOWLEDGEMENTS

Thanks to:TERRY BERRY, Local Studies Officer Oldham Metropolitan Borough; MARY J.PAINTER of Blackburn Central Library; THE LIBRARIAN, Ulverston Library; CHRISTINE STRICKLAND of Kendal Library; TIM ASHWORTH of Salford Local History Library. Special thanks to: MISS SUSAN WILSON of Lancaster Central Library, for her interest, enthusiasm and assistance with this project.

06197049

For
THE YOMPERS
Trish, Richard, Jaimie Lou and Lawly Liz
(with a little help from Martin)

Advice to Readers

Readers are advised that whilst every effort is taken by the author to ensure the accuracy of this guidebook, changes can occur which may affect the contents. It is advisable to check locally on transport, accommodation, shops etc but even rights-of-way can be altered and, more especially overseas, paths can be eradicated by landslip, forest fires or changes of ownership.

The publisher would welcome notes of any such changes

Front cover: Hampsfell Hospice

CONTENTS

1. Blacko Tower
2. Darwen Tower
3. Ellesmere Memorial
4. Hartshead Pike
5. Peel Monument
6. Rivington Pike
7. Ashton Memorial
8. Ashurst's Beacon
9. Billinge Beacon
10. Blackpool Tower
11. Jubilee Tower
12. Silverdale Pepperpot
13. Finsthwaite Tower
14. Hampsfell Hospice
15. Kirkhead Tower
16. The Ulverston Follies

INTRODUCTION

In this book we will embark upon a series of walks in which we will visit follies, prospect towers and curiosities in this most interesting of counties. We will walk over hill and dale, through woodlands and over sombre moors. We will also sample some of the more urban aspects of Lancashire's landscape, but above all, by the time you have completed all the "days out" in this book you will have gained an insight into and an understanding of the fascinating topography of north western England.

To many people, Lancashire means red brick cotton mills and Lowryesque industrial skylines. But this label is no more typical of Lancashire than the "muck and brass and cloth caps" image is of neighbouring Yorkshire. In fact Lancashire has a highly diverse landscape, well endowed with coyly hidden charms, which, unlike the more obvious natural wonders of Yorkshire, need to be sought out in order to be fully appreciated.

Lancashire is not what it was. Like Yorkshire it was altered by the local government reorganisation, which resulted in great chunks of its traditional anatomy being carved up and distributed elsewhere.

I have of course, cunningly ignored all these subtle changes. What today passes for "Lancashire" has no more ethnic reality than "Humberside". I would not seek to insult an "Owdham Mon" by referring to him as a "Greater Mancunian"! My Lancashire therefore is the Lancashire of old, Merseyside, Manchester and "Oversands" included.

Before Columbus people believed the world was flat. Before I went to college in Liverpool I believed the same of Lancashire. Not so. In reality Lancashire has more hills than flatlands. Passing over Blackstone Edge, the traditional gateway from the old West Riding into Lancashire, the vast basin of Greater Manchester falls away to the southwest. Into this basin empty numerous upland rivers, eventually joining forces to enter the Irish Sea via the River Mersey. This vast, predominantly urban area, stretching away to Warrington and the Cheshire lowlands, constitutes the greater part of "Flat" Lancashire.

Southeastern Lancashire flirts with the Peak District National

Park before giving way further northwards to the edges of the South Pennines. North of Rochdale the Pennines fan out westwards, running to the north of Greater Manchester, forming a high upland barrier twixt Mersey and Ribble, which reaches its climax on the moors around Belmont. This area is characterised by moors, industrialised valleys (like Rossendale), and roads which run largely north to south. Northwards again and we encounter the hills around Nelson, Colne and the Aire Gap, a westward running ridge which reaches its climax in the great whaleback of Pendle before falling away to the Ribble around Whalley. This is "Witch Country".

North of the Ribble the landscape changes. West of Clitheroe is Longridge and to the north of it the vast wildernesses of the Bowland Fells. Here the landscape is totally rural with sleepy villages where time seems to stand still. There are no industrialised valleys and little public right of access to the countryside.

As Belmont looks towards Preston, so the Bowlands look down on Lancaster, Lancashire's capital, dominating the mouth of the River Lune. The Lune rises in what was formerly Westmorland, in the Howgill Fells. North of the Lune, Morecambe Bay cuts deeply into the landscape, and much of what should be Lancashire is sands. Yorkshire and Westmorland loom large hereabouts, and Lancashire merely gets a strip of that complex geological cocktail of hills which lie twixt Morecambe Bay and the western fells of the Yorkshire Dales.

Lancashire's coastal strip is a rage of sand. The sandscape is at its grandest between the Mersey and Ribble estuaries. Formby, Ainsdale and Southport are characterised by vast, endless beaches backed by high dunes. On a busy day people appear as tiny, Lowryesque dots, and hazy vistas stretch from the Welsh Mountains to the Lakeland Fells. North of the Ribble, the Fylde, with Blackpool and its tower, is much the same. Beyond Fleetwood a quieter landscape stretches up to peaceful Glasson Dock and Sunderland Point, before the coast turns into the vast expanse of Morecambe Bay.

Oversands there is no real coastal strip. The rocky outliers of the Lake District descend abruptly to the sands of Morecambe Bay. On the far north western shore, Black Combe juts out into the sea behind Barrow-in-Furness, effectively blotting out any view along the Cumbrian coast. By this point, however, we have already passed beyond Lancashire's outer limits.

This then, essentially, is the distinctive topography of Lancashire. On our journeys in search of Lancashire's follies and curiosities, we will sample all of these landscapes to a greater or lesser degree. From Lakeland to the Mersey, from the South Pennines to Southport, Lancashire awaits.

Pilgrim's Cross Memorial, Holcombe Moor.
(East Lancashire 5)

ABOUT THE FOLLIES

Welcome to the oddities of Lancashire! There are fewer follies here than in neighbouring Yorkshire, but what they lack in number they more than make up for in quality. Indeed, it is Lancashire that is able to lay claim to a few superlatives - the tallest (Blackpool Tower), the biggest (Ashton Memorial), the most inaccessible (Ellesmere Memorial) and the most vandalised (Billinge Beacon).

Rambles and follies, I have found, do not always go together on the Lancashire side of the Pennines. Some follies are located in parks, or in the centres of industrial towns. This has sometimes raised a dilemma - the Ashton Memorial, for example, does not offer much scope for a country ramble and neither does Blackpool Tower, but such a book as this would not be complete without them. They are therefore included, even though there are no walks attached to them.

As in my other book covering Yorkshire, I have worked on the principle that the best things in life should be free (especially parking), and you will find that all the walks in this book are, as far as possible, designed with non-payment in mind. In this respect you will find that there are three types of follies - those you can get into, those you can't, and those you have to pay admission for!

This book gives the lie to the myth that Lancashire is a flat landscape filled with equally flat caps and belching mill chimneys. Lancashire's follies are predominantly prospect towers, and the prospects from them range from Lakeland via Merseyside and Greater Manchester, to the mountains of North Wales. Even this author, a dyed-in-the-wool Yorkshire nationalist, must concede that when it comes to views, the Lancastrians have got it sewn up. The views from many of Yorkshire's follies are excellent, yet nowhere do they compare with those of Lancashire for sheer visual range.

You will find that few of the rambles featured in this book are especially arduous, and indeed some of them are little more than pleasant strolls. On some you will find that the countryside is the major attraction, on others the architecture. Occasionally we strike lucky and get both. As in Yorkshire, it was not possible to base rambles around all the follies, and information about those not included you will find in the relevant Appendix.

Many years ago, when I was an emigré Yorkshireman in Liverpool, a fellow exile from Barnsley used to say that "'t'best thing abaht Lancasheer were t' rooad back ta Yorkshire!'" Hopefully this book will make amends for the insult. Anyway, on with your clogs, caps and shawls and let's explore the scenic delights of Lancashire!

Star Ratings

*	fair
**	good
***	very good

Stansfield Tower, Blacko.
(East Lancashire 1)

East Lancashire

1: BLACKO TOWER

Ghosts, "leggers" and witches are the main themes of this excellent walk on the bracing uplands twixt Pendleside and the Aire Gap.

Getting there:	Take the A56 Burnley-Skipton road to Foulridge, north of Colne. Turn onto the B6251 for a few hundred yards before bearing right down Warehouse Lane to the canalside, where there is a car park, shop and cafe.
Distance:	5 miles approx. Moderate
Map refs:	Start SD 888 428 Landranger 103
	Blacko Tower SD 859 422 Landranger 103
Rating:	Walk *** Follies and General Interest **

Foulridge is an ideal start for a ramble - an interesting little place, which manages to be both an industrial community and a rural backwater at the same time. Its fortunes were originally founded on woollen textiles, and many of the houses in its older parts belong to this period. Today, Foulridge's main asset is its position on the main Skipton-Burnley trunk road, but the village really owed its identity to the coming of the Leeds and Liverpool Canal at the end of the eighteenth century. This fact is readily acknowledged by the recent development for tourism of Foulridge Wharf.

Foulridge plays host to the canal's two main feeder reservoirs. Foulridge Lower Reservoir, also known somewhat exotically as Lake Burwain, was constructed in 1793, the canal wharf and warehouse being built somewhat later, in 1815.

The real wonder of Foulridge, though, is the mile long canal tunnel which runs to the north-west of the lake, and which (in the

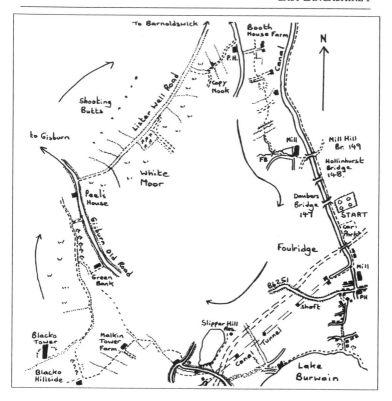

days before they changed the boundaries) carried boats from Yorkshire into Lancashire.

Before proceeding on our walk we must visit the entrance to the tunnel. Our walk visits both ends of the tunnel, and follows it on the surface for much of its distance. There is little to see at the Foulridge end. The intrepid will lean out from the iron rail set into the tunnel mouth, but all you are likely to see is darkness, and all you will hear is the eerie drip of dank waters. The surround of the tunnel mouth is carved with weird hieroglyphs, ornamentation made by the predominantly Irish navvies who constructed the canal.

The tunnel runs straight, but you cannot usually see the other end. I have seen it once from the "Lancashire" end, a tiny distant pinprick of light, but I did not see it on my last visit. The tunnel has subsided, as is evidenced by the roof height marker which hangs over the tunnel mouth. Perhaps this is a factor in obscuring the view.

I must confess to a love/hate relationship with the Foulridge Tunnel. I have navigated it twice - once in a small boat and once in a kayak. In a small boat it is fascinating and enthralling, in a kayak, with only a bike lamp for illumination, it is terrifying! The echo inside is phenomenal - every tiny sound is picked up, amplified and carried the full length of the tunnel. The yell when you crash into the wall in the darkness and narrowly avert a capsize, is carried up and endlessly echoed. The light from the airshafts brings a welcome respite, and as your eyes gradually adjust to the darkness, the far end gradually appears, a dirty yellow-green swirling blotch, small and distant beyond the dank mist that rises from the gurgling waters. When, with a sigh of relief you get into the "light zone" at the far end, the reflection of the tunnel roof in the waters becomes perfect, and you have the weird sensation of flying through the centre of an enormous tube.

The Foulridge Tunnel is unusual in that it was not bored but dug out from the surface, a deep cutting being excavated, roofed over and then buried. The tunnel was completed in 1796, although it was not until 1815 that the canal was completed along its full 127 miles. The tunnel has no towpath, and in the days before powered boats the horses had to be walked over the top, and the boat "legged" through the tunnel, a gruelling occupation involving lying on a special platform and pushing along the tunnel wall with your legs. There is now a one-way traffic light system, which operates on a time switch. In the adjacent Hole in the Wall pub, a photograph records a memorable incident in 1912 when a cow fell into the cut at the Barrowford end of the tunnel and swam right through to Foulridge, the exhausted animal apparently being revived with alcohol!

Our walk proceeds up through Foulridge, before following a footpath through housing to the shores of Lake Burwain. A pleasant footpath runs around the edge of the lake, and up on the distant hillside, Blacko Tower, the object of our walk, is in full view.

On the far side of the lake is haunted Hobstones Farm. The house

Foulridge Tunnel

has the unsavoury reputation of being one of the most haunted houses in England. Even its name is suggestive of something supernatural. "Hob" is an old Saxon word for hobgoblin, an evil troll or elf, and it is well-known that elves and fairies congregated at "the stones". There is reputed to be a prehistoric burial ground in the vicinity of Hobstones Farm, and even the reservoir - Lake Burwain - takes its name from an old English word meaning "burial ground".

Hobstones is essentially a fifteenth- or sixteenth-century farmstead which was entirely rebuilt in the eighteenth century. The property was once owned by the Parker family of Alkincoats near Colne, and there is a story that Colonel Parker, who was a royalist, once engaged in a short but bloody skirmish with a Parliamentary force at Hobstones during the Civil War. Since then people have supposedly seen a phantom troop of Roundheads crossing the nearby fields, fully armed with muskets and pikes. A more serious haunting at Hobstones, however, began back in the 1950s when a tenant farmer was quite literally caught with his pants down! He was sitting in an outside lavatory one morning when the door suddenly burst open and he was confronted by the figure of a dwarfish man, dressed in monk-like robes with a twisted face. He held out a bleeding arm, the lower part of which had been severed from the elbow. As the farmer sat there, frozen with horror and astonishment, the figure simply vanished.

There was no logical explanation for this apparition. Certainly no monastery ever existed at Hobstones, but there is a theory that some of the stone used in the eighteenth-century rebuilding may have come from Sawley Abbey, which was cruelly repressed during the dark days of the Dissolution.

The next spate of hauntings came in the 1970s, when the house was beset by poltergeist activity. There were bumps and thumps, objects moved inexplicably and a washing machine flung across the kitchen. Glass panes were shattered, smashed out from the inside, the glass ground to a powder. On one occasion a pile of rocks came tumbling down the stairs from the upstairs landing, from where they had come nobody knew, and on another a ghostly giant fist was seen pounding the front door. Matters came to a head on the night of 29th September 1974, when the house was shaken almost to its foundations by what the local press salaciously described as "wailing demons"! The Rector of Colne the Rev Noel Hawthorne was brought in, along with a skilled exorcist. Rituals were performed, holy water sprinkled and the hauntings progressively died down.

Our appetite for the supernatural whetted, we continue on our way, and having inspected the far end of the Foulridge Tunnel we proceed up the hillside to Malkin Tower Farm. Here yet more supernatural fare awaits us, for somewhere in the vicinity of this embattled farmhouse once stood Malkin Tower, the meeting place of the Pendle witches. The name "Malkin" is unusual and interesting, and research would suggest that the word means "scarecrow" or simply "untidy".

The actual location of Malkin Tower - the hovel where Old Demdike the supposed leader of the witches lived - has long been a subject of dispute. Some sources say it wasn't here at all, being actually located near Sadlers Farm at Newchurch-in-Pendle. Other writers speculate that it actually stood on the site of Blacko Tower, which we are shortly to ascend. Wherever it was, one thing is certain: on Good Friday 1612, a meeting was convened there of the friends and relatives of Demdike, Chattox, Anne Redfearn and Alizon Device, all of whom had just been sent to Lancaster Castle to await trial on charges of witchcraft. It was a fateful meeting which was to result in the arrest and subsequent condemnation of many of those who attended. It was not, as was alleged, a witches' feast - rather a gathering of fearful people, who having heard of the arrest of their relatives were desperately trying to decide what to do next.

It is not my intention to delve too deeply into the story of the Pendle Witches. The story is well known, and does not need to be retold by me. Our business is the discovery of follies and beyond Malkin Tower Farm our search is soon rewarded, for there, high above on our right we can suddenly see the gaunt outline of Blacko Tower.

Blacko (or Stansfield) Tower, (see page 11) a circular roughstone prospect tower was built around 1890 by one Jonathan Stansfield, a local grocer, who according to the story hoped to see over into Ribblesdale from it, only to find that when completed it was not high enough, and he was left with a useless "folly". One day in 1964 the sun rose over the hills to disclose a tower that had been mysteriously whitewashed during the night! Who did it, and why?? Many years ago a Bronze Age axehead was found near here, which was dated at about 3,500 years old. No one seems to know much about Blacko Tower - it is a place of mysteries.

Certainly people have had a few strange ideas about Blacko Tower. According to Guy Ragland Phillips, the antiquarian, the site is a point from which mysterious "straight track" alignments, or "leys", radiate in all directions. Apparently these tracks correspond to "earth currents" and may be detected by dowsing. I certainly did not feel any "vibrations" when I was there and neither, I suspect, did old Jonathan Stansfield.

The view from the tower is, as Stansfield found to his cost, not as extensive as one would like. Pendle Hill dominates the western prospect, and, as we already know, there is no view over into Ribblesdale. Southwards, towards the Nelson-Colne conurbation, there is an excellent prospect, but beyond the view is again blotted out by the Yorkshire South Pennines, ranging from Boulsworth Hill to Pinhaw Beacon. This does not detract from the tower, however, which for some mysterious reason seems to be excellently sited. There is the feeling that if there was no tower at this location, someone would almost certainly take it into his head to build one. And what of Stansfield's tower? A datestone over the tower bears the following biblical reference: PS 127 VI. The Psalm to which this refers is well known:

> Except the Lord build the House
> > they labour in vain that build it
> Except the Lord keep the city,
> > the watchman waketh but in vain

So was Blacko Tower built to satisfy the eccentric whims of a Lancashire grocer, or was there a more subtle purpose behind its construction? Was it perhaps a latter-day attempt to sanctify a pagan site, or to erase the suggestion that it was once a gathering place of witches? Who knows? Whatever the case, when the moon is full and the wind howls through the weathered stones, no doubt the shade of poor Stansfield haunts the turret, desperately trying to look over the hill to the sea, and to prevent the Devil from stealing his tower.

Our walk now proceeds back to Foulridge, but not by the same route we came. Beyond Peel's House, we follow an upland track along Lister Well Road, with heather moors on both sides and fine sweeping views towards the Aire Gap and, at the top of the rise, to Three Peaks country. Our descent to the canal (via a pint at the Fanny Grey) is not without interest, and there is a delightful ivy covered footbridge which we cross just above Mill Hill Bridge.

Our walk ends with a pleasant canalside walk back to Foulridge, which emerges by a most interesting limekiln. This particular specimen has (unlike most limekilns) been fully restored, and is one of a number of such kilns which were constructed alongside the canal at various points. These kilns were fed with limestone and coal in alternate layers, the lime and ashes being raked out from the grate at the bottom. The lime was used by farmers to sweeten sour land, and was also used in mortar. Many kilns were built by farmers for their own use. These canalside kilns however, were sited to take advantage of the fact that the Leeds-Liverpool Canal ran through both limestone and coal producing areas. Both were brought along the canal by boat to supply the kiln, and the resultant lime was sold at the kiln mouth, often being carried away in the same manner. In certain areas the kilns must have been an important facet of a busy canalside trade. The kiln at Foulridge, if its size is anything to go by, was obviously no exception.

And so we come to the end of what has been a most pleasant and interesting walk. If time permits, you could perhaps finish the day with an evening cruise down the canal, or simply a drive over to the Pendle Witch country. Whatever you do, you will take home the peculiar atmosphere of this haunted area - a place which despite the urban proximity of Nelson and Colne is still left alone with its strange memories.

The Walk

Start at Foulridge Wharf car park. After a brief detour to the tunnel entrance proceed up the road (Workhouse Lane) towards Foulridge, passing between factories. On reaching the Hole In The Wall Inn at the top of Towngate, turn right onto the B625 Barnoldswick Road for a few yards before turning off left between houses by a bus stop (A58). Pass a farm and houses, and on reaching a junction of roads bear slightly left and onwards, passing Edmunds Villa on the left

Lake Burwain

(Waller Hill). Continue onwards to Sycamore Drive passing Pasture Drive on the right. A signpost indicates the path which after crossing a tarmac road leads directly through trees down to the Foulridge Lower Reservoir (Lake Burwain).

Turn right, and follow the bank of the reservoir round to the Sailing Club. At the spillway bear right, passing a car park to the lane by Ball Bridge. Follow the Lane onwards, parallel to the canal tunnel (airshafts visible on the right). On joining a metalled lane by the old railway line turn right over a former level crossing. Turn left down a track and cross a small bridge to see the Leeds-Liverpool Canal emerging from the other end of the tunnel.

After inspecting the far exit of the Foulridge Tunnel retrace your steps to the lane. Turn left up the lane for a few yards, ignoring the signposted path which leads off right to Slipper Hill Reservoir. Instead proceed onwards until an unmarked stile on the left gives access to an indistinct path leading uphill to the left of the stream. Detour to the left of a modern stone-built house then continue onwards uphill, keeping the stream on the right and passing a footbridge before joining the Barnoldswick Road opposite Hollin Hall.

Cross the road and pass through the obvious stile opposite. Bear diagonally left through the field to a wallstile, then after passing through another stile follow the wall uphill a short distance before bearing diagonally left to yet another stile, which leads directly along the hillside to Malkin Tower Farm.

Pass through the farmyard and continue onwards towards Blacko Hillside Farm passing through three stiles. At the back of the farm buildings turn right following a stony gully steeply up the hillside. On reaching the top wall bear right to find a stile, beyond which turn left and pass by old quarry workings to reach the Stansfield Tower.

After exploring the tower retrace your steps to the stile. Now follow the wall onwards passing trees (right) to yet another stile, passing the white painted "Green Bank" on the right. Continue onwards until a short track leads off right between walls to the Gisburn Old Road.

On reaching the tarmac turn left, passing Peel's House on the left before bearing right through a signed kissing gate to a path which leads along the wallside, skirting boggy ground with a succession of plank bridges. Follow the wallside until another kissing gate gives access to Lister Well Road.

Follow the lane onwards passing a small plantation on the left and shooting butts on the right. On reaching the crest of the moor, where a fine view opens up towards the Yorkshire Dales, pass over a stile onto heather moor, following a well defined path which descends the hillside with fine views, before joining with the farm road by Copy Nook. Follow the farm road to reach tarmac at High Lane.

On reaching the road turn right, passing the Fanny Grey Inn on the right before passing through a signposted stile on the left. Descend the pasture to Booth House Farm, then turn right along the wallside (signed). Continue onwards to a stile which leads to old quarry remains, then pass through a succession of well marked stiles to reach a pretty little stone footbridge above a mill dam. Turn left, and follow a track down past the mill to a stile, beyond which a path leads directly to the canal at Mill Hill Bridge (no. 149). Turn right onto the canal towpath and follow it back to the car park at Foulridge.

2: DARWEN TOWER

On this walk you will encounter the finest prospect tower in Lancashire, a mysterious wishing well, woodlands, nature trails, sombre moors and sweeping views in all directions. Pick a clear day to enjoy the far reaching panorama.

Getting there:	From Blackburn follow the A666 towards Darwen. Turn off right at Earcroft then left at the crossroads, following the lane up to Tockholes. Continue onwards to the Royal Hotel, and park in the car park by the Roddlesworth Information Centre.
Distance:	5¹/₂ miles
Map ref:	SD 667 215 Landranger 103
Rating:	Walk ** Follies and General Interest ***

The walk out to Darwen Tower is predominantly a moorland one, a moorland distantly crowned by the tower itself. Darwen Moor is characterised by heather, the remains of old mines and a succession of bench seats. The seats emphasise the public nature of the moors, for the opening up of Darwen Moor marked one of the earliest victories in the struggle for walker's rights of access to open country.

During the 1870s and 1880s there was a continuing battle between local campaigners and the lord of the manor, who had taken it upon himself to close off the moors to public access. A man by the name of John Oldman attempted to organise a mass trespass, but this had little popular support. In July 1878 the protesters precipitated a war when they overpowered the gamekeepers, which resulted in a writ to answer in the High Court in London. Oldman was chosen to represent the protesters, and had to use his pocket watch as security in order to get a loan to attend the proceedings. The court decided in favour of the Freedom Movement, and an agreement was eventually made to open up twenty five acres of moorland as urban common, and to allow public use of all footpaths

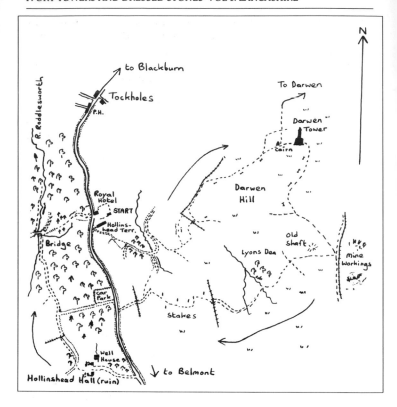

and roads. On 6th September 1896, a throng of thousands ascended the moor to celebrate the grand opening. Walking here today, on a sunny Bank Holiday Monday, you might be inclined to think that little had changed since then.

Darwen Tower is one of those rare follies that really is as good as it looks, and does not reward your uphill toil with a bricked-up entrance door or sealed-off upper gallery. A wide stone staircase winds up to a viewing gallery part way up the tower. For many follies that might be an end to it - but not in the case of Darwen Tower. The staircase continues on up the folly, eventually giving way to an iron newel staircase reminiscent of those that used to exist on old tramcars. A vandal proof perspex door gives access to the viewing turret. You heave it open and the wind howls and buffets down the staircase - and this is a pleasant day!

Now for some vital statistics. Darwen Tower is an octagonal structure with outer faces 15 feet wide. It contains 65 stone steps and 17 iron ones. Its outer walls are 2 feet thick and it has been recently extensively restored. The architecture has a pseudo-Tudor feel about it, a feeling reinforced by the arches and shield panels at the base of the tower. The left one of three panels over the northern archway informs us that:

1897

THIS TOWER

Was erected (and a sum of £650 devoted in aid of
the Nursing Association) by the public subscriptions
raised to commemorate the Diamond Jubilee
of the reign of

HER MAJESTY
QUEEN VICTORIA

Foundation Laid June 22nd 1897
By Alexander Carus Esq.Mayor:
Opened September 24th 1898 by

THE REVD WILLIAM ARTHUR DUCKWORTH M.A.
LORD OF THE MANOR
CHARLES PHILIP HUNTINGTON J.P.

The centre panel bears an ornate shield celebrating the diamond jubilee, whilst the right hand panel bears a hard-to-read list of the names of members of the jubilee committee. Behind these mosaic tablets hangs a tale.

Our story begins in 1897, when an anonymous letter writer with the pseudonym "Landmark" first suggested building a tower in the columns of the *Darwen News*. He ventured that not only would it be a good way to mark the forthcoming jubilee, but would also be a monument to the victory of local people in their recent battle to win access to the moors. Later in that same year the idea was raised yet again, when it was decided to raise money for the local Nursing Association, which sent sick poor people to convalescent homes. At the end of the meeting a Councillor Shorrock proposed that part of the funding might be used to erect a Jubilee Tower at Red Delph Quarry, using the abundant supply of stone that could be found there.

A competition was held for the best design. There were twenty one entrants, but in the end the princely prize of £5 went to Mr David Ellison of the Darwen Borough Engineer's Office. The tower site and stone from the delph were donated by the lord of the manor, the Rev W.A.Duckworth, a magnanimous gesture on his part considering the recent argument over public access.

The jubilee was celebrated on the 22nd June 1897, when a public holiday was declared all over the Empire. In Darwen the first sod was cut for the tower by the Mayor, Alexander Carus. The pleasant summer's day ended with a bonfire and firework display.

Needless to say, the actual building of the tower proved to be a far more formidable undertaking than had been envisaged by its founding fathers! It had been hoped that it would cost around £400 - but they were way off the mark. Consequently more and more money for the tower was diverted from the Nursing Association funds, a process which soon drew complaints from the local community. In the end the money was simply divided equally and a tender for £773 3s 5d was accepted for the job from local builder Richard J.Whalley. Progress was slow and marred by inclement weather, and even on the official opening day (24th September 1898) the porticoes at the bottom of the tower were still incomplete.

This time the Rev Duckworth himself officiated at the ceremony, as thousands of people ascended the hillside to where a rostrum had been erected for the speakers. By 3.30pm more than 3000 people had arrived, many of them from other parts of Lancashire. Music was provided, speeches made and votes of thanks given, these latter being twice interrupted by the band, which seemed obsessively intent on repeating the National Anthem ad nauseam! And so the tower was opened to the general public, a symbol not only of the diamond jubilee, but also of the freedom of the moors.

Since then the folly has had a chequered history. The original turret was made of pitch pine bolted to iron girders, surmounted by a lead dome, a ball finial and an ornate weather vane. This was blown away in a gale on the 5th April 1947. Afterwards it was decided that the tower should be left as it was - a fatal decision for a folly. From then on it was a downhill spiral. Blackened by smoke, wrecked and defaced by vandals, by 1962 the council were embarking upon stage three in the life of a folly - bricking up the entrance. It looked like the tower was doomed to oblivion.

The reprieve came in 1971 when Councillor Dr Bill Lees was made mayor, and announced his intention of seeing the tower cleaned, repaired and fitted out with a new turret. He established a fund for this purpose, and raised over £2,500. In March 1972 the council were informed that the tower, along with the India Mill Chimney in the town below, had been listed by the Department of the Environment as being of special architectural and historical interest.

In the end the tower was restored, £3000 being raised by public donations and materials being supplied by local industry. On Sunday 18th June 1972, the tower was officially re-opened by Alderman Edwin Yates, Freeman of Darwen. Despite the inclement weather, over 200 people attended the opening, and Councillor Lees, his mission accomplished, thanked all who had helped to give Darwen back its Jubilee Tower.

There is a postscript to the story. On 16th October 1972 the Darwen General Purposes and Development Committee received a letter from one Hiram B.Lansky of St Louis, USA, offering to buy the tower for £250,000 in order to take it down, stone by stone, and rebuild it on his ranch. The offer turned out to be a hoax, but the resultant uproar resulted in a genuine enquiry, this time from an organisation in Missouri. Needless to say, Darwen declined the offer and the tower remains in its rightful home, belaboured by Pennine wind and rain.

Despite pretexts like jubilees and victories we all know the real reason for the construction of a prospect tower - so people can enjoy the view. Like most of Lancashire's towers, the views from Darwen Tower are excellent indeed, particularly to the west. If the viewfinder on the top is to be believed, a clear day will reward you with the following prospect:

SE	-	Kinder Scout, Holcombe Moor
E	-	Boulsworth Hill, Rombalds Moor
NE	-	Great Whernside, Pendle, Penyghent
N	-	Ingleborough, Whernside, Longridge Fell,

Wardstone Fell, Langdale Pikes, Coniston Old Man
NW   - Black Combe, Blackpool Tower, The Isle of Man
W   - The Ribble Estuary
SW-S - Southport, Great Orme, Snowdon

Certainly Pendle Beacon and Blackpool Tower are usually visible, as is the neighbouring Jubilee Tower on Holcombe Moor. The view eastwards tends to be largely obscured by the South Pennine watersheds around Rossendale, however, and you will find the best prospect is usually to the north-west.

We have said much about the tower, but little about Darwen's other major architectural curiosity, the India Mill Chimney, which lies in the valley below. Modelled on the Campanile in Venice, it was built (along with the mill) for Shorrock Brothers cotton spinners in 1867. The chimney is built of local Cadshaw stone. The mill originally opened amid great celebrations, an event described in the local paper as "A new era in social history".

Our route does not actually descend into Darwen. Instead, we eventually head south-westwards, towards the great mast at Belmont which looms large on the near horizon. The remains of old mine workings dot the moors hereabouts, as we proceed towards Lyons Den which is now little more than a few trees standing sentinel over a pile of stones. Lyons Den was named after John Lyon, a seven foot high giant who apparently constructed a simple house of turf and heather here around 1790. The story goes that when three local men went to visit him, they saw him crawling out of the lowly entrance to the hut on all fours. One of them called out "See... he's coming out of the Lyons Den!" The name stuck.

From Lyons Den we descend to the Tockholes road, a left turn giving access to a track which leads to the sad ruins of Hollinshead Hall. Like many once fine Pennine houses, it has been reduced to little more than a pile of stones. The hall was almost entirely rebuilt in 1776, being further altered during the last century (though no doubt there were older buildings on the site). Many pictures and drawings still exist to show us what the house looked like in its heyday.

Hollinshead Hall was once the property of an ancient and distinguished line, with roots stretching back to the Middle Ages. Ralph Holinshed of Cophurst, the famous chronicler who among other things provided the source for Shakespeare's *Macbeth*, and who died in about 1580, was a member of this illustrious family. Certainly it was not until 1761 that the Hollinsheads actually appeared on the scene, when John Hollinshead purchased the Manor of Tockholes from Sir George Warren, of Poynton, Cheshire. By the 1840s, Hollinshead Hall had become the seat of Henry Brock-Hollinshead Esq who married in 1845 and died in March 1858. Thereafter the house remained empty and deteriorated to the pile of stones it is today - a sad demise for a once fine house.

The real curiosity here, however, is to be found tucked away in a corner of what once must have been the hall's fine gardens. Some seventeenth-century style seats and masonry around a small paved yard guard the entrance to a curious stone vaulted building, the dim interior of which contains a most tantalising spring, its waters issuing from the mouth of a stone lion's head. The Hollinshead Hall Wellhouse has to be one of the least known treasures of northern England. It is so remote and obscure that few outsiders are even aware of its existence. (Indeed the author only stumbled upon it by accident.) This building is a jewel, and if the history of Hollinshead Hall has given rise to confusion and debate, attempts to unearth the history and purpose of its Wellhouse have resulted in out-and-out controversy!

The Wellhouse is essentially a low building with a stone-flagged roof, the appearance of which both inside and out suggests that it was built sometime during the seventeenth century. The internal ornamentation, though crude, displays hints of the classical baroque. The floor is paved, with a central channel, and there are stone bench seats to either side. To the left and right of the main well are stone cisterns, and the whole building has the appearance and aspect of a baptistry chapel, which it almost certainly was at one time.

Debate has raged in the past as to whether this was a wishing well or a holy well, but a folklorist would say that it was probably both. It must almost certainly have been consecrated at some time, but any sacred well would have been revered long before Christianity came on the scene. The Hollinshead well would almost certainly have been dedicated to a saint, probably St Helen. According to Twycross writing in 1846, the well was formerly called "The Holy Spring" and was frequently visited by pilgrims who came for the water, which had a reputation for curing eye ailments. He also informs us that out of the lion's head flow the waters of five different springs. This latter point is significant: a single outpouring of five springs would be regarded as sacred by pagans, being the manifestation of a water goddess. This was perhaps the original reason for its veneration.

The interior of the wellhouse is vaulted, a surprise not hinted at by the stone flagged roof outside. The vault looks older than the rest of the building, and is possibly fifteenth century, this original "cover building" being itself covered by the present structure. The seventeenth-century shell was probably built by the Radcliffes, who like many persecuted Lancashire "recusant" families were keen to protect the heritage of the Roman church. Perhaps a priest officiated here, conducting adult baptisms in the "male" and "female" cisterns on either side of the well. Masses may also have been celebrated here. This hypothesis makes a lot of sense. Here, tucked away secludedly in what is even now a remote and obscure location is a purpose-built Catholic baptistry with a pre-reformation authenticity which, if challenged by the authorities, could be simply dismissed as a baroque garden ornament.

This is my view. Other writers have suggested that the wellhouse was built in the last century, was merely a buttery, a garden ornament or folly, or even the cell of an early Christian hermit, possibly an associate of Paulinus!

The rest of our journey is a pleasant amble through woodlands, eventually walking alongside the River Roddlesworth, or the "Moulder Water" as it is sometimes known. The beck slides peacefully down to Halliwell Fold Bridge (note the name - "Halli" or "Holy" well); and from here a pleasant path up through the woods leads back to Hollinshead Terrace and the start of our perambulation. A drink in the adjacent pub should ensure a pleasant end to a pleasant day.

The Walk

Start at the car park by the Royal Hotel and the Roddlesworth Information Centre. Turn left onto the road and then, passing the end house of Hollinshead Terrace, pass through a rusty old kissing gate to follow a track up the lower slopes of Darwen Hill. At the first gate join a track which passes under trees and at the next junction ignore the track leading onwards and instead wind around to the left over Stepback Brook (which is channelled beneath the high banking which carries the track). A few yards on double back sharply to the right, following a well defined path which winds back up the hillside, passing a ruin on the left. At the remains of a seat, high above a cascade in the stream, turn sharp left, following the path which leads to a fence stile on the moor edge. Continue onwards, following a well defined route which leads past a succession of seats before reaching the Jubilee Tower.

From the tower, follow another well defined path which winds around the contours of the moor to the south. There are more seats, and an area of wet ground. At the next junction of tracks, by yet another seat, turn left and walk onwards a short distance to reach a fence above the remains of old coal workings. Do not follow the continuation of the path along the hillside, but instead turn sharp right, ascending steeply up the moor, eventually passing an old mineshaft on the right (not obvious - a grassy hollow - like a shakehole). Beyond a junction of four paths and a stile, a green track leads onwards to cross two streams upstream of the trees and ruins of "Lyons Den". The route bears to the right, up to another stile, beyond which there is a steep descent to the road, following a succession of waymarked posts.

On reaching the road, bear left, and continue for about a quarter of a mile before turning right along a track which leads to the ruins of Hollinshead Hall. After visiting the Well House with its wishing well, pass through the ruins and follow a well defined track which bears right, up the hillside. At a junction of tracks continue onwards (the right-hand track leads back to the road and a car park), descending through woodlands, to reach the River Roddlesworth on the left. On reaching the bridge over the stream, do not cross it, but instead turn right up steps, passing through a corridor of coniferous trees. The path crosses a small footbridge before eventually becoming a track in a gully which leads without complication back up to the road and the start of the walk.

3: THE ELLESMERE MEMORIAL AND WORSLEY

On this pleasant walk on the urban fringe of Manchester we encounter boats, canals, woodlands, a lake with wildfowl, an excellent (if inaccessible) folly, and visit Worsley Delph - the cradle of the Industrial Revolution.

Getting there:	M62 to Junction 13. From roundabout, take first junction off towards Winton. Turn right into car park just before reaching the bridge over the canal (the Packet House is on your left).
Distance:	4¹/₂ miles approx.
Map ref:	Ellesmere Memorial SD 735 009 Landranger 109
Rating:	Walk ** Follies and General Interest ***

Worsley is the cradle of the Industrial Revolution, and a suburb of Salford. These statements might lead you to think that it is a depressingly grimy sort of a place, yet nothing could be further from the truth.

Worsley is delightful. Yes, much of it is a built-up area, and there are numerous busy roads, but it is not those images which linger in your memory. What remains rather is a vision of gentle woodlands, timbered Tudor-style buildings and the tranquillity of the Bridgewater Canal, with its orange waters and beautifully-adorned canal boats.

Our perambulation starts and finishes by the canal. The local council have recognised the historical significance of the area and have obligingly provided a history trail marked by large noticeboards that outline the story of the area. These are illustrated and are of great interest.

The story of Worsley is essentially the story of two men, the one an eccentric aristocrat and the other a half-literate Derbyshire millwright. According to the legend, lovesick Francis Egerton, the third Duke of Bridgewater, having broken off his engagement to the

The well-house at
Hollingshead Hall
and (inset) the interior

The Wilkinson obelisk at Lindale

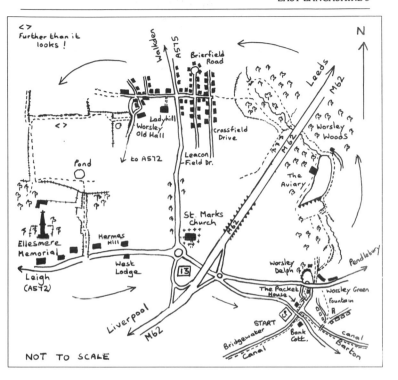

NOT TO SCALE

Duchess of Hamilton, decided that he would devote the rest of his life to commerce. To do this he engaged James Brindley, a millright, to construct a canal that would take the coal from his Worsley mines to the markets of Manchester, and by so doing constructed Britain's first artificial waterway and unwittingly launched the Industrial Revolution.

So much for the legend. The truth, however, is somewhat less romantic. For one thing Egerton was no lovesick fool. His works in Worsley were already well underway before he broke off his engagement. As to his canal being the first modern man-made waterway, this is also not strictly correct, for the Sankey Brook navigation near St Helens had already claimed that distinction in 1751.

The rest, however, is basically true. Egerton had a problem, and he solved it with great ingenuity. It was only seven miles to Manchester, but to transport coal there by packhorse was inefficient and expensive. Egerton realised that the only answer was a "navigation", and after removing potential opposition by getting a private act passed in Parliament, the duke finally began work on his Bridgewater Canal.

The rest is history. He employed James Brindley (whom he never properly paid for his services) to construct the canal. Brindley was semi-literate, and had no experience of waterways, but was a man of great intelligence and engineering genius. The canal was (and still is) supplied by water from Bridgewater's mines, and during the course of its journey to Manchester it crossed the Irwell by the Barton Aqueduct - an incredible feat of engineering for the time, and the wonder of the age. The canal was completed in 1765.

So to our walk. The first place of interest we encounter is the Boathouse on the opposite side of the canal. This was built by Lord Ellesmere (Bridgewater's great nephew) to house a royal barge especially constructed for Queen Victoria's visit in 1851. The boat was pulled by two grey boat horses, one of which, being nervous, shied and fell headlong into the cut!

Beyond the Boathouse we cross the canal via the hump backed footbridge which was built by Lord Ellesmere in 1901. We cross tranquil Worsley Green, surrounded by its Tudor-style cottages to take a look at The Fountain, essentially a red-brick structure containing an urn. Few people would imagine that 200 years ago this peaceful spot was an industrial eyesore, for the green was originally the works yard, criss-crossed with tramways, and the fountain was the base of a smoke belching factory chimney. The yard was demolished in the early 1900s, and the surrounding cottages built soon after. The Fountain commemorates the duke and his achievements and carries an inscription in Latin which Henry Hart Davies translated in 1905 as follows:

> A lofty column breathing smoke and fire,
> Did I the Builder's glory once aspire,
> Whose founder was that Duke who far and wide
> Bridged water through Bridgewater's countryside.
> Stranger! this spot, where once did never cease

Great Vulcan's year, would sleep in silent peace,
But beneath my very stones does mount
That water's source, his honour's spring and fount.
Alas! that I who gazed o'er field and town,
Should to these proportions dwindle down.
But all's not over, still enough remains
To testify past glories, duties, pain.

Crossing the green to the main road, we bear left and soon arrive at Worsley Delph, which, more than anywhere else, was the birthplace of and raison d'être for, the Bridgewater Canal.

Worsley Delph, as its name suggests, was originally a quarry. Sandstone from the delph was used in the construction of Brindley's canal. The marks of the quarrymen's picks and the shot-holes for their explosives may still be seen in the sheer walls of gritstone. An arm from the Bridgewater Canal leads directly into the delph, and the whole area has been made into a substantial canal basin. At the base of the cliff, two low and spidery-looking tunnels disappear underground. Like the basin itself, the tunnels are partially silted up, and slimy looking orange water trickles out of one of the entrances. This is caused by particles of ochre (iron hydroxide) being leached out of the rock, and it discolours the canal for a great distance. These uninviting-looking archways were the adits from the duke's mines, being the source not only of the duke's coal but also of a substantial water supply to feed the canal.

Yet they were more than this. For beyond these low arches exist marvels of engineering unsurpassed by even the Bridgewater Canal itself. The duke, having planned the canal which would connect the markets of Manchester to the coal heaps of Worsley, decided he would go a step further, and extend it to the underground coal face itself.

This amazing system of subterranean waterways was begun in 1759, soon after the excavation of the Bridgewater Canal. It was largely the work of the duke's overseer, John Gilbert. The twin tunnels we see in the delph unite after about 500 yards and lead into a labyrinth of canals which are around fifty-two miles in extent and constructed on four levels. These extensive stygian highways extended into the Worsley coalfield even as far as Walkden and Farnworth, connecting into and draining most of the mines in the area. How, you might ask, was it possible to have a usable canal operating on four different levels? John Gilbert's answer was both simple and ingenious - underground canals led to the top and bottom of a dry incline and, using a system of trolleys, pulleys and locks, the weight of a laden boat descending under gravity drew the arriving unladen boat up the incline. The passage of the boats along the adits was assisted by sluice gates, which opened to release the build up of water behind them, creating a wave which propelled the boat along.

The duke's underground canals ceased to carry coal in 1889, but the tunnels were regularly inspected right down to the 1960s as they drained other mines in the area still operating. Today they are left with their memories and the ghosts of the duke's miners - men, women and children, who laboured in the darkness for up to fourteen hours a day crawling on hands and knees in dim candlelight. Theirs was the real achievement, and it should not be forgotten.

Beyond Worsley Delph we come to the real treat of our walk - Worsley Woods. This extensive area of woodland contains nature trails, a lake with wildfowl and picturesque cottages, and passes beneath that more recent feat of engineering, the M62. The woods were originally owned by the duke and then by the first Earl of Ellesmere, who planted much of the woodlands and created the network of footpaths. It was the earl who constructed the Old Warke Dam for fishing and boating, and the lovely house known as "The Aviary".

From the woods, we pass through an uninteresting housing estate and cross a busy road before reaching pleasant countryside once more by Worsley Old Hall. This is now a restaurant, but was originally the centre of the duke's operations. After the duke died in 1803, his estates eventually passed to Francis Leveson-Gower, the second son of the Marquis of Stafford. In accordance with the duke's will, Francis adopted the name of Egerton, and in 1846 was created the Earl of Ellesmere. The earl was a well known philanthropist, and it is to his monument, which stands just across the fields, that we now proceed.

The Ellesmere Memorial is at once a delight and a disappointment. Seen at a distance, a tall Gothic spire surrounded by trees, it looks good, and no doubt it is good. The only trouble is there is no way you can get to it! On the road side it has been completely cut off by housing, and on the other side it has been completely sealed in by steel fencing and pony paddocks.

My immediate reaction when faced with a situation like this was to write the whole thing off. But then I decided I would write about it anyway, if only to draw public attention to the plight of the folly. For here is an ornate and interesting piece of local history which is being allowed quietly to fall down, out of sight and out of mind. There is no public access to it, and, it would seem, no private access either. No doubt the shade of Lord Ellesmere is even now turning in his grave!

Over in neighbouring Worsley we have seen history trails, nature trails and a developing tourist attraction, yet here, just a short distance down the road, we are witnessing the triumph of private property over national heritage. There is an increasing awareness all over Britain of the irreplaceable architectural heritage embodied in follies, and happily, although many have been lost, many others have been saved before it is too late. But here in the Ellesmere Memorial is a unique structure that is about to disappear.

The Ellesmere Memorial was built in 1859 to commemorate Francis Egerton, the first Earl of Ellesmere, whose death had been greatly mourned by those who remembered him for his good works in the 1840s when he had found work for cotton operatives whose families would otherwise have starved. He had also done much to improve the area, providing parks, playgrounds and public woodlands.

The memorial was conceived by a committee of local worthies, who set up a subscription fund, which raised £1,800 towards its construction. A competition for the best design was announced, with a first prize of 60 guineas, and the winning design was by Driver and Weber of London. The winner of the third prize, a Mr Keeling, submitted designs for "a columnar composition, in three stages, of the Doric and Tuscan orders, Height 90 feet." The whole structure being capped by a glass dome, silvered like a looking glass!

The foundation stone for the memorial was laid on November 17th, 1858. An illuminated manuscript bearing the names of all the dignitaries involved in the project was sealed in a cavity in the

Ellesmere Memorial,
Worsley

masonry - a time capsule for posterity. The completed Memorial was opened on 10th August 1860, when it was formally presented to the son of the late earl by Mr Fereday Smith, chairman of the monument committee.

The Ellesmere Memorial is an ashlar structure incorporating a band of Minton encaustic tiles and corner columns of "the new serpentine discovered at the Lizard". The building has two main stages and a spire, which originally stood atop a tall octagonal column, since removed. The corners of the building bore heraldic finials, which were removed around 1980. The memorial is 132 feet high, and contains a spiral staircase of 125 steps. An inscription, surmounted by the arms of the earl, explains the purpose of the tower: "An affectionate tribute to the memory of Francis Egerton,

First Earl of Ellesmere, K.G., from the tenantry, servants, carriers and others connected with his landed and trading interests, 1860."

At the top of the monument there is room for six people, and a view which on clear days is said to range to Cheshire and Flintshire. The balcony is bounded by iron railings. Years ago, the Ellesmere Memorial was a popular local attraction, especially on Good Fridays when local people made an annual pilgrimage here to ascend the tower and enjoy the wide ranging views from the observatory at the top. Today those glories have passed, and the only visitors to the Memorial are the birds, which are undeterred by the surrounding fencing.

And so we approach the end of our perambulation, which leads us back to Worsley Delph along the busy main road, passing the first Earl of Ellesmere's main architectural contribution to the area, the magnificent neo-Gothic St Mark's Church, which contains the earl's tomb. Soon we are back on the canal by the Packet House, a picture postcard sort of a place, originally built in the eighteenth century. From the steps at the front of the Packet House, the Duke of Bridgewater once ran regular passenger services to Runcorn, Warrington and Manchester, a slow, uncomfortable, yet highly popular mode of transport until eclipsed by the advent of the railway age. Here is a place to picnic, relax, and reflect upon the great achievements (and evils) which were created by the Industrial Revolution; triumphs and tribulations which are still echoed in the present day. For right or wrong, for better or worse, here, in this leafy suburb of Greater Manchester, the modern world began.

The Walk

Start at the car park in Worsley. Turn right over the canal then right again by Bank Cottage, descending steps to the canal towpath. Turn right under the bridge and follow the towpath round to the footbridge. Turn left over the footbridge to the Fountain on Worsley Green. Bear left over the green to the main road. Cross the road and pass some Tudor styled shops and a restaurant to the seats and information board overlooking Worsley Delph.

Ascend steps up into the woods then bear right, following the stream up to the dam, passing to the right of the lake and The Aviary. Continue onwards to a mock Tudor cottage, where a lifebelt

The Packet House, Worsley

stands forlornly among boggy woodland! Leave the track and follow the path up the wood to the tunnel under the M62. Beyond the motorway cross the stepping-stones over the stream (on left). Ascend the slope via some steps, then turn right onto a nature trail footpath which leads further up the wood. Near the top of the wood an unofficial "shortcut" leads off left to a fence, beyond which a beaten trod crosses a field to enter housing on Crossfield Drive at its junction with Woodlands Road.

Proceed along Woodlands Road to its junction with the busy A575 main road. Cross the road, and continue along the road opposite to Worsley Old Hall, passing stables on the left.

Just beyond Worsley Old Hall Turn right, passing through a gate onto a grassy track which skirts a pond on the left before leading along the side of the hedge (on right) to a junction of paths. Bear left, then at the woodland boundary turn left again, passing alongside a fence with the Ellesmere Memorial in view on the right, shrouded by trees. When a pond appears on the left turn right onto an overgrown footpath which leads between houses to emerge into the main Leigh Road (A572), just beyond Hermes Hill.

Turn left, and proceed for about ³/₄ mile along the road to the roundabout and St Mark's Church. Continue onwards to the bridge by Worsley Delph, then turn right down steps into a narrow ginnel, crossing the canal arm to the front of The Packet House. Cross the main road to the car park opposite.

(Note: If you wish to avoid the short cut simply continue alongside the motorway from the stepping-stones in Worsley Woods, eventually turning right into Crossfield Drive, behind St Mark's Church. Follow it over the rise, passing through the housing estate, then turn left onto Woodlands Road.)

4: HARTSHEAD PIKE, MOSSLEY

A quaint old pub, an overgrown reservoir and a highly distinctive folly tower characterise this fine walk with sweeping views over Oldham and Greater Manchester.

Getting there:	From Oldham (Mumps Roundabout) follow A669 to Grotton. At junction turn right onto A6050 towards Mossley, joining the A670 coming in on the left. Follow A670 uphill past Mossley, and just beyond the church on Mossley Brow, turn sharp right onto Broad Carr Lane. Turn left onto rough track and park by the Collier's Arms.
Distance:	3 miles. Easy.
Map ref:	SD 962 026 Landranger 109 or Peak District tourist map
Rating:	Walk ** Follies and General Interest **

> On Owdham Edge the grass is green,
> reetest view that ere tha's seen
> if tha stands on top an tha looks about
> ther's nowt but mill wi' ther chimney spouts
>
> *old song*

Hartshead Pike has a character all its own. Situated on an upthrust of land between Mossley and Southern Oldham, it crowns the last gasp of the Pennines, standing at the point where the hills give way to the low-lying industrial landscapes of Greater Manchester. The distinctive red-brick chimneys and dominating hulks of Lancashire's cotton mills are also in evidence, though now not so numerous and all pervading as when Lowry captured their character for all time.

East of Hartshead Pike lies Mossley and the Tame Valley leading northwards to Uppermill. This area, generally known as Saddleworth, is a finger of gritstone Yorkshire protruding into red-brick Lancashire. Eastwards of Mossley the hills rise steeply into the bleak moors of the Pennine watershed, but here at Hartshead Pike the landscape is hilly yet rather more subdued.

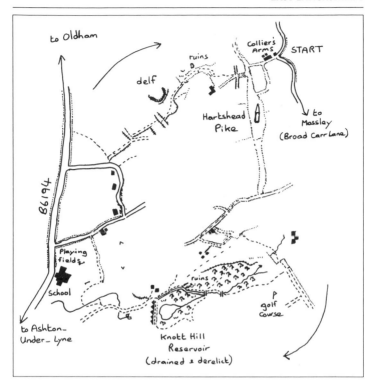

Hartshead Pike, sometimes known as Heartshead Pike or Tower, is a tall circular building with a conical roof. It was originally intended to be 85 feet high, but no doubt sights had to be lowered when the bills began to come in. The tower's history is chronicled by a number of inscriptions:

> Look well at me before ye go
> and mind ye nothing at me throw
> This Pike was Rebuilt By
> Pub-lick Contribution:Anno:Do:
> 1751

AND
RE-ERECTED
BY PUBLIC SUBSCRIPTION
TO COMMEMORATE THE MARRIAGE OF

H.R.H ALBERT EDWARD, PRINCE OF WALES
TO H.R.H THE PRINCESS ALEXANDRA OF DENMARK
And to restore
THE ANCIENT LANDMARK OF
HARTSHEAD PIKE

THE RT HON GEORGE HARRY 7TH EARL OF
STAMFORD AND WARRINGTON
BEING LORD OF THE MANOR ARTHUR F PAYNE ESQ STEWARD

THE FOUNDATION STONE WAS LAID BY SAMUEL DUNCUFT LEES
M.D.
MAYOR OF THE MANOR
SEPT 17th 1863 JOHN EATON ARCHITECT

The site of the original Hartshead Pike stands at 925 feet above sea level, upon what was almost certainly once the site of a beacon cairn, which was lit to warn of invasion. Tradition says that the first tower to be built on this spot was a hunting stand built for King Canute! Another story relates that Henry II once witnessed a tournament here which was put on for his benefit by the Baron of Ashlynne.

It seems likely that the first tower was probably built late seventeenth or early eighteenth century, but there is no evidence to uphold or refute this view. What we do know is that the tower was rebuilt in 1751. This 1751 tower was damaged by lightning in 1794 and progressively fell into ruins. By the middle of the nineteenth century, nothing was left of the old pike except for the large foundation stones, circular and sixteen feet in diameter, which today may still be seen a short distance to the north of the present tower.

The present pike, as the inscription informs us, dates from 1863.

Hartshead Pike, Mossley

It was built in the wake of the hardship caused by the drying up of Lancashire's cotton supply due to the American Civil War. It is quite possible that much of the labour on the building was performed as "relief work" by cotton operatives. It was proposed that the tower would be rebuilt to celebrate a forthcoming royal marriage, and that a subscription list be opened up to pay for it. This was done, and by September 1863 about £230 had been raised. As the inscription states, the foundation stone of the present pike was duly laid, and a hermetically sealed time capsule bottle containing coins, copies of Ashton's newspapers and an explanatory parchment was buried beneath.

In 1912 the pike, along with its hilltop, was given to Hartshead Parish Council, but by the end of the First World War it was falling once more into disrepair. A little shop had been established in the ground floor of the pike, selling pop and sweets for a ha'penny, and visitors could (belching mill chimneys permitting) ascend the tower and enjoy the sweeping views.

In January 1928 the pike was seriously damaged by a great storm. Already it had been suffering from the attentions of "the rough lads of the district" who "think it fair game to make it a target for every kind of missile, and it has been treated very roughly in this respect". The parish council did not have the money to undertake repairs, so a public fund was set up with the intention of raising £500. Thus was the pike restored to its present state.

Leaving the pike our walk descends to the nearby golf course before entering the woodlands around the remains of the Knott Hill Reservoir. Here is a water catchment that has been drained and allowed to fall into dereliction. On the steeply shelving stone-lined bed, where once the deep waters lapped, there is a vast forest of young birch trees. In the bottom of the reservoir is a dank rubbish-filled pool, frequented by the odd angler. There are fly tips, motor bike erosion, graffiti and a general air of urban decay. In 1988 the North Western Water Authority had plans to fill the site with industrial waste, but after an eight months long campaign by the Hartshead Action Group the authority finally agreed to transfer the site to Tameside Council for development into a conservation area. Certainly the area has potential as a country park - it is already being used as one.

Beyond Knott Hill Reservoir our walk becomes a leisurely stroll along playing fields and a country lane, finally culminating in a pleasant ascent of green, boggy pastures which lead unerringly back to Hartshead Pike.

Now all that remains between you and your car is landlord Charlie Mills and the Colliers Arms, which, more than any other hostelry in the area is most definitely a place not to be missed! The Colliers Arms is an old-fashioned pub. Essentially it is the beershop front of an old farmhouse surrounded by a retinue of scrap vehicles and rickety old sheds. You can peek through the mullioned windows in to two old pub rooms - each one characterised by flagged floors, low oak beams, planked settles and cast iron tables. Two old pianos, a black leaded fireplace and faded original 1930s wallpaper complete the scene. The pub is tiny - so much so that on a Sunday lunchtime most of the customers are obliged to sit and drink on the wall across the road! Here is a rare survivor of those moorland drinking dens that gave so much delight to the pre- and postwar generations. Visit the Colliers Arms today, for tomorrow it might not be there. This walk should help you work up a suitable thirst.

The Walk

From the Collier's Arms follow the track round to the left and bear right up a path between walls. At the top of the path turn left, following an obvious track up to Hartshead Pike. From the Pike continue onwards until a lane is joined. Turn right and follow it down past a farm. Just beyond, (before the next farm) pass through a stile on the left, and follow a shattered wall to a second stile. Turn left, to join a path which leads right to another stile and a junction of paths. Ignore a path leading right towards a pylon and instead bear left then right down the hillside following an indistinct path which leads over the beck to a track leading along the edge of the golf course.

On reaching the golf course turn right, following the edge of woodland to where a waymarked stile (not obvious) gives access to the wood. Follow the bank of the stream for a few yards then cross it over a slab bridge. The path leads to a white fence, and the stream enters a catchwater drain. Here a choice of routes can be made all of which lead around the edge of the drained and tree-filled Knott Hill

Reservoir. At the outfall of the catchwater drain proceed down the dam to a track (which becomes cobbled). Where the track bears to the left, follow a path which descends steeply to the stream. Ascend the little wood and bear right to a stile, then follow a well defined path along the edge of playing fields, passing a school on the left.

At the tarmac lane by a stile turn right then first left, following the lane until it veers sharply to the left, by modern luxury houses. Take the second waymarked path on the right, bearing right up the hillside to a waymarked post. Continue up the hillside, following waymarked signposts, passing through stiles and boggy ground and skirting the edge of a quarry working before joining a track between shattered walls by ruins. Where a holly choked track bears right towards housing, proceed diagonally across the field towards a post on the skyline. Cross the track and follow the path between wall and fence which rejoins the track to Hartshead Pike. Turn left then right, following the track back to the Collier's Arms.

Colliers Arms
Mossley

5: PEEL MONUMENT, HOLCOMBE MOOR

A fine upland ramble on the Pennine Moorlands with sweeping views leading to an excellent prospect tower which is sometimes open for inspection. En route you will encounter the site of an ancient cross, an old well and the scene of a gruesome murder.

Getting there:	Follow M66-A56 to Haslingden (west of Rawtenstall) turning left onto the B6214, heading southwest to Helmshore, where there is limited parking opposite the Memorial Gardens. (Note the fine clock tower.) Helmshore has all mod cons - inn, post office, shops etc. - as well as an interesting textile museum at Higher Mill. If you wish to cut out the ramble and visit the Peel Monument direct, continue along the B6214 on to Ramsbottom and park below the monument near Holcombe Church, where there is a car park.
Distance:	9 miles approx.
Map refs:	Start of walk SD 782 208 Landranger 103 Peel Monument SD 777 165 Landranger 109
Rating:	Walk ** Follies and General Interest **

Our walk to the Peel Monument lies exclusively in the Lancashire part of that area of Pennine uplands which have been loosely dubbed the South Pennines. This is something of a misnomer, for while the area may be geographically much the same as Yorkshire Calderdale just over the hill, ethnically it might as well be in another dimension.

Rossendale, once a leading centre of felt making, still has the largest concentration of slipper and footwear factories in any one place, and until quite recently was an area of grimy chimneys and increasingly derelict and decaying factories. Behind this industrial blight the area contains some fine walking country, but it is only recently that walks hereabouts have ceased to be the preserve of locals.

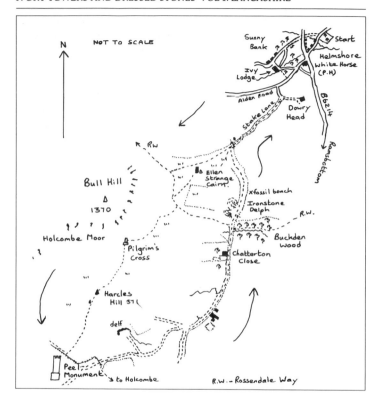

Now this has changed. The tourism "virus" which so drastically changed the face of "mucky" Hebden Bridge over in Yorkshire has spread up the Calder Valley to Todmorden and has spilled over into hardheaded Lancashire.

And so we embark upon our walk, passing first by the site of Sunny Bank Mill where, in 1866, Joseph Porritt began his papermaker's felt business. Porritt, like most Lancashire entrepreneurs, made his mark on the landscape in a substantial way, eventually owning most of the Alden Valley and having mills stretching from one side of the Irwell Valley to the other. For a long time the Porritts dominated the papermaker's felt trade. Inevitably, as time went on, Porritts was swallowed up by larger business concerns. Decline set in, and by 1977 the whole complex had been demolished, an ignominious end to almost a century of local history.

Before reaching Tor Side House, which was Porritt's residence, we turn sharp left by Ivy Lodge to Alden Road, and thence up Stake Lane, passing Dowry Head on the left. A boggy ascent, made all the more so by the passage of motorcycles, leads upwards to the edge of the moors and Robin Hood's Well, a tiny spring of uncertain origin, and not the only well of that name to be found in the Pennines. Stake Lane was once a part of the old Pilgrims Way to Whalley Abbey, and it is probable that the well was intended as a place of refreshment for weary travellers. Did Robin Hood come here? It seems unlikely. Robin Hood places occur all over the North of England, and it is possible that "Robin Hood" was but a pseudonym for the Green Man, a very ancient pre-Christian deity who would later become a symbol of Saxon resistance to Norman aggression. An old northern expression speaks of having "Robin Hood's choice"- ie. no choice at all! Perhaps this was the only refreshment stop available to the traveller crossing the moor - hence the name. When I visited the well it was dry!

Beyond the gate we take to the open moorland, bearing left to a cairn and a curious upright stone in the heather. It bears the letters "E S" and a curious, badly-weathered sculpture depicting a female figure, with the faint outlines of others. The initials stand for Ellen Strange, and the stone marks the spot where, in 1735, she was most foully murdered.

The story goes that Ellen once lived with her parents at Ash Farm, Hawkshaw. She fell in love with a pedlar from Stone Fold named Billy, and one day they set off to Haslingden Fair together. On their way home they called at the White Horse in Helmshore, and were seen to go off home together. It was the last time she was seen alive. Ellen was murdered at this remote spot, where her body was found. The pedlar was arrested and confessed to his guilt. He was executed at Lancaster Castle, and his body afterwards hanged in chains on nearby Bull Hill. The cairn and stone were subsequently erected by sentimental visitors to this sad and lonely spot.

Passing the wall corner we ascend the moor to the boundary of the MOD danger area on Bull Hill. Soldiers are not new hereabouts, sometime during the Civil Wars a band of Royalist soldiers camped up on these moors. From the edge of Bull Hill a well defined path leads around the perimeter of the training area (marked by posts), descending to the squat monument erected on the site of the Pilgrims Cross.

The inscription is self explanatory, even if you have to walk all around this windswept monument to read it:

> ON THIS SITE STOOD THE ANCIENT PILGRIMS CROSS. IT WAS EXISTING IN AD 1176 AND PROBABLY MUCH EARLIER. PILGRIMS TO WHALLEY ABBEY PRAYED AND RESTED HERE
>
> IN AD 1176 AND IN AD 1225 THE PILGRIMS CROSS IS NAMED IN CHARTERS OF GIFTS OF LAND IN HOLCOMBE FOREST. IN AD 1662 KING CHARLES II GAVE THIS MANOR TO GENERAL MONK DUKE OF ALBEMARLE FROM WHOM IT HAS DESCENDED TO THE PRESENT LORD OF THE MANOR
>
> THIS MEMORIAL STONE WAS PLACED HERE MAY 24th 1902 BY THE COPYHOLDERS OF THE MANOR AND OTHERS
>
> NOTHING IS KNOWN OF THE REMOVAL OF THE ANCIENT CROSS BUT ITS MASSIVE SOCKET FOUNDATION STONE REMAINED HERE UNTIL AUGUST 1901.

Some old sources refer to the cross as Chattertons or Whowells Cross. The 1902 monument we see now was largely the result of the enthusiasm of the Revd H Dowsett, Vicar of Holcombe, who desired to preserve the memory of the ancient cross, the last vestiges of which had been destroyed by vandals in 1901. One marvels at the tenacity of those turn-of-the-century hooligans whose enthusiasm for malicious destruction brought them out to this remote and godforsaken spot.

So we proceed along the heathery moortop to the summit of windblown Harcles Hill, looking back briefly to the now distant Pilgrims Cross, a tiny forlorn dot, lost and lonely in the middle of a vast wasteland. Having said our goodbyes, we descend steeply to the Peel Monument on Holcombe Moor.

Peel Monument

The Peel Monument or Holcombe Moor Tower is one of the great landmarks of East Lancashire. It looks out southwards over the vast urban sprawl of Greater Manchester. Seen from the M66 on a murky day one might be forgiven for thinking it a gaunt chimney, yet here, seen at close quarters, this blackened, castellated tower is obviously no such thing.

A single word over the entrance reveals the reason for its construction. The Peel Tower was erected to the memory of Prime Minister Sir Robert Peel, who, among many other achievements, was responsible for founding the police force and repealing the much-hated Corn Laws, which kept the price of bread at an artificially high level. Peel was born in Bury in 1788, where there is a statue to his memory.

The tower was erected at a cost of £1,000 using stone quarried from the hill on which it stands - without the consent of the landowner. The tower was opened on 9th September 1852, the ceremony being conducted by one Joshua Knowles of Stormer Hill, the proprietor of Tottington Calico Works. A special train was laid on from Salford to Ramsbottom especially for the ceremony, but by the time it arrived all the proceedings were over. The tower was at first managed by a local trust. In 1868 the landowner, the Duke of Buccleuch, granted a lease on Holcombe Hill, including the tower, for the sum of 7/6 a year. The trustees were allowed to charge admission to the tower and sell light refreshments.

As with most follies, in the twentieth century the tower has had somewhat of a chequered career. By 1929 it had fallen into a decayed state, and £2,500 had to be raised to replace the rotting wooden staircase with an iron one and generally to renovate the structure. In the 1930s it was run by a local farmer, Percy Vickers, who supplemented the family income by opening up the tower to the public. During the war the tower became a Home Guard lookout post, and by the late 1940s it was observed that the iron staircase had become badly rusted. Consequently it was closed to the public in 1947, and in 1949 possession passed from the trustees to Ramsbottom District Council. In 1950 the exterior was repointed, but otherwise the tower was left sealed up. It looked like its days were numbered.

But Lancashire looks after its prospect towers. Like its neighbours at Rivington and Darwen, the Peel Monument has benefited from the recent restoration boom. With grant assistance, a new concrete staircase was constructed and the tower repointed. After being sealed up for thirty-eight years, the tower was once again re-opened to the public in 1985.

The tower is now administered by the Metropolitan Borough of Bury, and is open at weekends and bank holidays. When I arrived, a union flag was fluttering from the flagstaff, which was visibly bending in the gale force wind. At the foot of the tower a local brass band was in full throat, desperately trying to play whilst at the same time trying to prevent their sheet music from flying over into Yorkshire! The tower itself is an adventure. Inside there is a small cafe which sells booklets and refreshments, but it is the ascent of the tower itself which fascinates. As you ascend the concrete steps, the deep stairwell on your left appears increasingly horrendous! The tower is in fact 128 feet high, and when the final section of the climb suddenly turns into a steel spiral staircase running out over the stairwell your feeling of vertigo is complete. The tower originally contained 148 steps, but this modern flight, by the reckoning of my daughter, contains 157 steps, 23 of which are spiral.

Outside, on the top of the tower, you feel you are going to be blown off your feet, but the view is impressive enough, particularly over Greater Manchester. With a little concentration you should be able to make out Hartshead Pike and the transmitter tower in Heaton Park. To the north-west Darwen Tower is visible, as is Belmont, but the area to the west is effectively blocked out by the moorlands. Eastwards there are fine views over Rossendale and across Rochdale to Blackstone Edge, but the high Pennine watersheds effectively rule out any peeking into Yorkshire! The view is really of Manchester, with sweeping views across that great basin to the moorlands of the Dark Peak.

Chilled by the wind, eyes streaming and with the feeling that the tower is actually moving, we descend back to the relative comforts of the café. In the base of the tower are a number of inscriptions. One, a painted board, simply tells us about the history of the tower, whilst the other, an inscribed piece of marble placed in the tower during the 1929 restoration, quotes from Peel's 1846 resignation speech:

PEEL MONUMENT HOLCOMBE
ERECTED 1852
IN MEMORY OF SIR ROBERT PEEL

It may be that I shall leave
a name sometimes remembered
with expressions of goodwill
in the abodes of those, whose
lot it is to labour, and to earn
their daily bread with the sweat
of their brow - when they shall
recruit their exhausted strength
with abundant and untaxed food
the sweeter, because it is no
longer leavened with a
sense of injustice.

EXTRACT FROM SPEECH
OF SIR ROBERT PEEL, DELIVERED
IN THE HOUSE OF COMMONS
JANUARY 27th 1846

And so, with this fine sentiment in mind, we take to a well-defined track leading along the hillside above the church, from which we are able to enjoy the fine views over the valley to nearby Ramsbottom. Ramsbottom once had its own magnificent folly in the form of Grant's Tower, a bizarre (and massive) Gothic structure erected by William Grant of Grant Bros, at the time the chief manufacturers of Ramsbottom. The folly was intended to commemorate his father's journey from Morayshire to Lancashire in 1783 in search of work. Unfortunately Grant's Tower was brought down by a great gale in 1943, and Nuttall Hall, the Grant residence, was demolished by the council in 1952. The philanthropic Grant brothers, William and Daniel, built mills and cottages all over the valley, frequently importing workers from as far afield as London and Hull. They were immortalised by Dickens in Nicholas Nickleby as benevolent Ned and Charles Cheeryble, although Dickens set them in London. St Andrews Church, which was opened in 1834, is a fine example of their originality and ingenuity. It was originally heated by hot air supplied from Grants Square Mill that came up the hillside through a brick flue almost a quarter of a mile long. The kindly Grants have still left their mark on Ramsbottom, even though most of their more magnificent undertakings are now gone.

Our route eventually leads us past Chatterton Close to a pipe and cascade at the top of Buckden Wood, beyond which lie the spoil heaps of Ironstone Delph - once the site of an early primitive stone/clay furnace. From here the track leads up the hill back to the junction of walls by Robin Hood's Well, at the top of Stake Lane. From here, we head

Robin Hood's Well

back to Helmshore and the parked car, a fitting end to a fine tramp over lonely windswept moors.

The Walk

Start at Bridge End by the Memorial Gardens at Helmshore. Follow Sunnybank Road under the bridge, passing the site of Sunny Bank Mill. At the fork go left along a cobbled track, and at the next junction (Ivy Lodge), cross and enter the field opposite through an iron kissing gate. The field path ascends, passing a telegraph pole, and passing to the right of trees, before passing through a second kissing gate into Alden Lane. Turn right up the lane, then left again up the narrow (signed) lane leading to Dowry Head. At the entrance gates turn right, following a wet and muddy track (Stake Lane) up the hillside to Robin Hood's Well.

Beyond Robin Hood's Well, pass through the gate and follow the right hand path up the moor (wall on the right). Bear slightly left, following an indistinct route over wet moor to the cairn and memorial to Ellen Strange.

From the cairn proceed over the moor to the wall corner and follow the obvious route up to the MOD Range warning notices. If flags are not flying, follow the footpath which contours the hillside, passing a series of red-and-white striped posts on the right. The path winds round to the right as the view to the west opens up, and proceeds without complication to the Pilgrim's Cross.

From the Pilgrim's Cross follow a well defined (and boggy) route along the ridge to the summit cairn on Harcles Hill. Descend the hillside, cross a small stream then cross over a fence to reach the Peel Monument.

From the Peel Monument a well defined track leads back along the edge of the moor before bearing right to a junction of tracks. Bear left, along Moor Road, passing two farms (second one Chatterton Close) before reaching the old workings at Ironstone Delph, just beyond the pipe and cascade at the top of Buckden Wood. From Ironstone Delph the track leads onwards without complication to rejoin the outward route at Robin Hood's Well. Follow Stake Lane back down to Alden Lane which leads down to the White Horse Inn. Turn left, crossing the road opposite the junction and take the right-hand road fork, which leads back downhill to Helmshore and Bridge End.

6: RIVINGTON PIKE

Overgrown ornamental gardens, woodlands, reservoirs, bleak moors, a sham castle and two prospect towers are all to be found in this most magnificent of country parks. Rivington is Bolton's Playground and Lancashire's chief jewel. You must take the kids!

Getting there:	Awkward, but easy enough. From Bolton follow the A673 to Horwich. Beyond the roundabout turn right between gateposts into Lever Park. Great House Barn stands to the left of the Horwich-Rivington Lane.
Distance:	5 miles approx.
Map ref:	SD 628 138 Landranger 109
Rating:	Walk *** Follies and General Interest ***

Rivington is one of the great playgrounds of Northern England. Here is where Lancashire folk come to picnic, to walk, and to enjoy the peaceful countryside and the wooded glades. On a pleasant summer Sunday you will find the whole area alive with visitors. Don't let this put you off however, as there is room for everyone. You get a bit of everything at Rivington: reservoirs, parkland, woodland, moorland, overgrown ornamental gardens, waterfalls and lakes, and of course (I almost forgot) follies - three of them to be exact.

For all of these natural (and not so natural!) wonders we may thank one man, a man whose vision, benevolence and desire for escapism quite literally created the landscape we see here today. His name was William Hesketh Lever, and, among his many other accomplishments he was probably one of the last of Britain's great folly builders.

William Hesketh Lever was born in September 1851 at 16 Wood Street, Bolton. His father was a wholesale grocer and a strict chapelgoer. Lever was educated in Bolton, and at the age of fifteen began work for his father, for the princely sum of one shilling per week! One of his many tasks was to cut soap to customer's

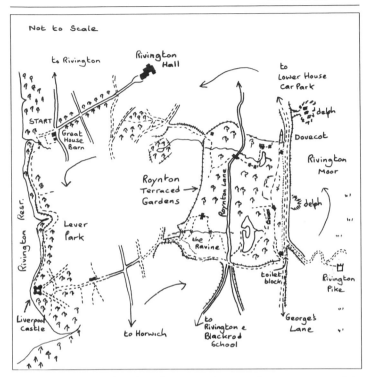

requirements. By the time he was nineteen he was engaged in obtaining orders from retailers in the Bolton area, and he served the business so well that in 1872 his father made him a partner in the firm. In 1874, Lever married and settled in Park Street, Bolton.

As business expanded, Lever was appointed manager of new premises in Wigan, and very soon Lever & Co had become one of the largest wholesale grocers in the North-west. Lever's secret was the use of what in those days was quite a novel idea - advertising.

Yet Lever went further. He was to invent something that would eventually become quite ubiquitous - the Trade Brand. Lever wanted to create a product with his own distinctive trademark that no-one could copy. The product he chose was soap, and the name he decided upon was Sunlight. Sunlight Soap was launched with an intensive advertising campaign. The name even appeared on the back of postage stamps! Where soap had been traditionally cut to demand, Lever bought it direct from the manufacturers, had it stamped, cut into individual standard measures and packaged. It proved to be an instant and phenomenal success.

A large factory was opened near Birkenhead in 1889. Lever decided that he wanted to house his ever expanding workforce near the means of production, so he began work on a model village with lawns, wide roads and spacious houses, each with its own garden. This village he called Port Sunlight, and by the standards of the time it was positively luxurious!

By 1900, Lever had created an empire, with factories in Europe and America. When he died in 1925, weighted down with honours, Lever had £50,000,000 in issued capital and over 100,000 employees.

William Hesketh Lever, Lord and later Viscount Leverhulme, did not forget his humble Bolton origins, neither did he desert the town and the Lancashire people he had always known so well. At various points in his career he was Liberal MP for the Wirral and the Lord Mayor of Bolton. He established museums and churches, he endowed universities and schools, amassed a large art collection and gave public lectures in which he advocated a six hour day for industrial workers.

Yet Lever's abiding interest was in landscape design and architecture, a pastime in which he indulged at every available opportunity. He purchased the Rivington Hall Estate in 1899 for £60,000, and it proved to be the ideal place in which to give this passion for landscaping a free hand.

At Rivington, Lever created Britain's first ever country park in the modern sense of the word. Forty-five acres below Rivington Pike he kept back for himself but the rest he donated to Bolton Corporation in 1902 for the enjoyment of the general public. Lever converted two barns into refreshment rooms, turned the hall into an art gallery and populated his paddocks with exotic animals. He laid out roads, avenues - and follies. Lever Park was officially opened on 18th May 1904 with a further ceremony in 1911 to celebrate the completion of the building work. The two obelisks by the entrance to the park were erected after Lever's death.

Our walk begins at Great House Barn where there is a car park,

Rivington Terraced Gardens

a café and an information centre. This barn reputedly dates back to Saxon times, but has been much restored, first in the 1700s and then by Lord Leverhulme. The roof is held up by two huge crucks, which are essentially the two halves of a tree sawn down the middle with tie beams held together by wooden pegs. The barn, along with its sister Great Hall Barn is thought to have once been a tithe barn, where a "tithe" or tenth of the local grain produce was stored for the upkeep of the clergy.

From Great House Barn our walk proceeds to the shores of Rivington Reservoir. This was built between 1852 and 1857. It is part of a chain of reservoirs which were originally constructed under the Rivington Pike Scheme to provide water for Liverpool's thirsty masses. The reservoirs in the Rivington area hold around 4,000 million gallons, and still supply Liverpool with around 11.5 million gallons of water a day.

So, having walked along the lakeside we come to Lord Leverhulme's first great folly, Liverpool Castle, a sham ruin. The original Liverpool Castle once stood on the site of the present Queen Victoria Statue in Derby Square, Liverpool. It was demolished in 1720 to make way for a church. Lord Leverhulme began work on his replica around 1911-12, and work continued on it right down to 1930. The architect was reputedly Thomas H.Mawson, the landscape gardener who laid out the park and with whom Lever enjoyed a fruitful working relationship, but it seems more than likely that most of the design work was done by Lever himself. The castle was never completed, but perhaps it was never intended to be. Maybe it was meant to be a sham ruin from the outset. It also has a ghost - quite an achievement for a twentieth-century baronial castle. It is reputedly haunted by a white-robed figure, as witnessed a number of years ago by five council workmen who watched it for over two hours as it glided around the castle precincts.

Our route proceeds along one of the Lever Park avenues before heading up the hillside towards the Roynton Gardens. Here were the 45 acres Lord Leverhulme reserved for himself - his private pleasure gardens. Work began here in 1900 and continued in various phases right down to 1925. During the Second World War the gardens passed to the War Office before eventually being bought by Liverpool Corporation Waterworks, during which time they became dilapidated and overgrown - and remain so, although sections of undergrowth have now been cut back and paths waymarked to create a Terraced Gardens Trail. A map of this trail is available at the information centre.

It is hard to describe the Terraced Gardens. There is nothing anywhere quite like them. The whole area is one of overgrown terraces, grottoes, loggias, arches and steps, a jungle labyrinth of ornamental pathways leading along and up and down the steep wooded hillside. It is a folly hunter's paradise. Our route joins the gardens at the Ravine which was constructed in 1921 to designs by T.H.Mawson, a seemingly chaotic jumble of man-made waterfalls, footbridges, stepping stones and rockpools, cunningly contrived to look as natural as possible. Nearing the top we arrive at the overgrown remains of the Japanese Garden, perhaps Mawson's greatest creation, laid out in 1922 and undoubtedly inspired by Lord Leverhulme's visit to Japan in 1913. In its heyday it featured teahouses, waterfalls, lanterns and an ornamental lake, as well as a vast variety of exotic trees and shrubs. All of this is now buried beneath scrub and rhododendrons.

Reaching the top of the gardens, we come to a track running alongside open country, and beyond it a further track which winds up the hillside to the summit of Rivington Pike. The pike, which is about 1,200 feet above sea level, is the oldest folly you will find at Rivington, being constructed for one John Andrews in 1733. Why he built it is not known. Like most builders of follies he probably built it merely to make his mark on the landscape - or to mark out the boundary of his estates perhaps. The tower is 17 feet square and 20 feet high, and has a faintly Babylonian appearance. In the days before it was walled up, it had a wooden roof, four windows, a fireplace and a cellar. Shooting parties from Rivington Hall once used it as a shelter. Perhaps, like the folly at the base of Roseberry Topping in North Yorkshire, it was constructed with that purpose in mind. In 1902, when Liverpool Corporation purchased the pike from Lord Leverhulme, they proposed demolition, but such was the public outcry they were forced to desist, consequently donating the tower to Chorley Rural District Council in 1912. Today the tower is protected as a grade two listed building.

Of course Rivington Pike, like many prospect tower locations, has long been a site of topographical significance. It was once part of the beacon chain and may have been in use as such as early as the twelfth century. The Rivington Beacon's neighbours were Ashurst's Beacon and Billinge Beacon, both of which are visited in this book. It is recorded that on the night of 19th July 1588 the beacon was lit to warn of the Spanish Armada. Other beacons have been lit on Rivington Pike since those turbulent times. The coronation of George V, the ending of the First World War, Queen Elizabeth's silver jubilee in 1977 and the royal wedding of 1981 have all resulted in celebration bonfires on the pike.

The view from the pike, like all the landmarks on these western hills, is excellent. The Lancashire coast, Blackpool Tower and Southport's gasometer are usually in view, as is Ashurst's Beacon and, if you are lucky, the power station at Heysham. The prospect eastwards, however, is blocked off by the great bulk of Winter Hill with its Belmont TV transmitter. On a exceptionally clear day you should be able to see the Lake District, the Isle of Man and the Welsh mountains.

The landmark plays host to the Pike Race and the Pike Fair. The first Pike Race was held in 1892, and has been regularly run since. It is held on Easter Saturday and is entered by hundreds of runners. The race starts from the entrance to Lever Park. The Pike Fair, too,

Rivington Pike

is still observed. It is held on a Good Friday and attracts large crowds. Last but not least, there is reputedly a spectral horseman in the vicinity of the pike, but you are unlikely to see him on a busy bank holiday!

Descending the pike, we retrace our steps back down to Lord Leverhulme's gardens. A short stroll and we soon arrive at the open terrace that was once the site of Roynton Cottage, his private bungalow. Little remains now except for a few tiles in the grass. The first bungalow to be constructed on the site, in 1901, was a temporary prefabricated affair built of timber which, despite the description, was luxuriously appointed, and surrounded by beautifully-laid-out lawns. The bungalow was intended to be used for shooting weekends and short visits. Its life was somewhat short-lived, however, for on the night of 7th July 1913 it was deliberately burnt down by Edith Rigby, an active suffragette, while the Levers dined with King George V, Queen Mary and the Derbys at Knowsley. The whole thing must have been a shock, for Lady Lever died just three weeks later.

Undaunted, Lever built a second Roynton Cottage, this time in

The Ashton Memorial, Lancaster

Roynton Gardens, Rivington
Liverpool Castle, Rivington

stone, and at a cost of £30,000. It was completed in 1914 and a few years later a magnificent circular ballroom was added, with a 44 feet diameter sprung floor of oak parquetry and a glass domed ceiling. Leverhulme's dome was designed by R.Herman Crook and depicted the stars as they appeared on the date of Lever's birth. All this, along with the three entrance lodges, was demolished by Lever's old adversary Liverpool Corporation in 1948, in the face of massive public opposition.

And so we arrive at what must surely be Rivington's finest folly - the 1910 Pigeon Tower or Dovecot. This was designed by T.H.Mawson as a piece of Scottish baronial fancy. Lord Leverhulme had interests in the Hebrides, and his Scottish aspirations are perhaps reflected in the architecture of this tower. It is said that the top floor of the tower was used by Lady Leverhulme as a sewing room, where she could enjoy the views. The lower two floors apparently housed the pigeons. By 1975 the tower had become little more than a ruined shell, but it has now happily been re-roofed and restored at a cost of around £5,000, yet another lucky beneficiary of the 1980s fashion for conserving old buildings.

From the Dovecot we descend steps - lots of them. The whole descent is one of terraces, balustrades, arches, paved causeways and loggias - all overgrown. Soon we arrive at the swimming pool, a murky pond where Lord Leverhulme once used to take his morning dip; and beyond we descend through rhododendrons to emerge on top of the Seven Arch Bridge over Roynton Lane which was built in 1910, and reputedly designed by Lever himself. Beyond we bear left, then right, eventually leaving the gardens by the site of the South Lodge, which, before it was demolished, had a thatched roof.

And now we near the end of our journey as our route descends back to Lever Park, joining a tree lined avenue to the left of Rivington Hall. Here was where Lord Leverhulme had his art gallery. The present hall is largely Georgian with nineteenth-century additions, although there has reputedly been a manor on the site for almost 1,000 years. The fine red-brick west front was built by Robert Andrews in 1774, but there are earlier fragments as evidenced by a lintel in the west wing dated 1694.

From Rivington Hall we follow a wide avenue back to Great

House Barn and the car park. This is the end of our follies perambulation, but by no means the end of what Rivington has to offer. A right turn along the road leads on to Rivington village, where an early Unitarian chapel dating from 1703 and a Tudor church (1540) are but two of the attractions on offer. For the energetic there is the orienteering course, the Anglezarke Woodland Trail, and for the would-be industrial archaeologist there is a trail to Lead Mines Clough. These walks also tie in with the Roddlesworth Nature Trails which we touched upon in our visit to Darwen Tower. For the folly hunter wishing to combine interest in follies with marathon walking there is a Three Towers Walk which connects Rivington Pike with Darwen Tower and the Peel Monument on Holcombe Moor. All this information is locally available. Rivington, you will find, is an enchanting place.

The Walk

Start at Great House Barn. Follow the track down towards the Reservoir, passing the short stay car park and children's playground on the left. At the woodland boundary turn left, following paths which lead along the side of the reservoir to the sham Liverpool Castle.

From the castle take the central of the three approach avenues. (This is not immediately obvious. If you are on the correct one, Rivington Pike should be in view slightly to your right.) The avenue leads directly to the main road. Cross the road and continue onwards, passing Gilsbrook on the right. Cross a tree-lined avenue and bear slightly left uphill. Soon the post of orienteering checkpoint A appears on the left. Bear right, passing through two successive gates, each of which offers a choice between a stile or a kissing gate.

Beyond the second gate turn left over the stream into the Terraced Gardens. The path winds up the hillside through rhododendrons, eventually meeting stone steps ascending to the right. These lead to the Breres Meadow Shelter (no.4 on the "Terraced Gardens Trail"). Ascend steps and turn right along the paved path above to a stone footbridge over the "Ravine" (posts 5 & 6).

Beyond the bridge bear sharply left up steps, following waymarks for the Terraced Gardens Trail. At the top of the steps turn right, noting a series of grottoes on the left. The path winds up the hillside

The Dovecot, Rivington

before winding sharply left to emerge into Roynton Lane by post 8.
Cross the lane and ascend steps, passing Lantern Base (post 8) then turn right to the Japanese Lake (post 9). Cross the concrete

bridge at the lake outfall then (following way-marks) bear left, passing above the lake. At a junction of paths (by post) ascend steps to post 13.

Now turn left, passing ruined buildings and posts 13,14,12 and 15. At post 16 turn right up steps to find post 17, by two rounded gate pillars. Now ascend part of "The Long Walk", passing under an archway by post 19. Beyond the arch bear right to the shelter by the site of the former Tennis Courts (20). Ascend the shelter steps to the next path up (there is a post). Now turn right, (leaving the Terraced

Liverpool Castle, Rivington

Gardens Trail), and wind left up a short flight of steps, before turning right onto a level path which leads out to a gate at the edge of the gardens. Turn left, ascending a flight of wooden steps alongside the boundary fence, to emerge into George's Lane at the top of the gardens. Turn left to the toilet block.

Opposite the toilet block a well defined track and stone steps lead up to the summit of Rivington Pike. After visiting the Pike retrace your steps to the toilet block. Re-enter gardens along the wide path to the left of the toilet block. This leads to the site of The Bungalow and the Circular Ballroom (posts 22 & 23). From here the path leads onwards to the Dovecot (post 29).

From the Dovecot, essentially follow the Terraced Gardens Trail back to Great House Barn. After descending various flights of steps turn left, passing the swimming pool on the left before descending right down the Garden Shelter Steps to Lever's Bridge spanning Roynton Lane. Beyond the bridge and arch turn left, descending steps and crossing various paths before encountering a sign which directs us sharply down to the right. From here the path leads without complication to the South Lodge Entrance.

Continue downwards to the next gate at a junction of tracks then onwards, following a path through the woods, which joins a second track near Rivington Hall. Turn left, sharply right, then left again to follow the tree lined avenue which leads down to the road and the Great House Barn.

N.B. For a more detailed map of Lord Leverhulme's overgrown gardens see leaflet *The Rivington Terraced Gardens Trail* available from Great House Barn café - price 15p. This will help you find your way around The Labyrinth!

West Lancashire

7: THE ASHTON MEMORIAL, LANCASTER

Simply the biggest folly in Britain - Lancashire's answer to the Taj Mahal.

Getting there:	Located in Williamson Park, due east of Lancaster town centre. Take the Trough of Bowland road towards Hornsea Pottery.
Map ref:	SD 494 615 Landranger 97
Rating:	Follies and General Interest ***

Lancashire can lay claim not only to Britain's biggest prospect tower on the golden mile in Blackpool, but also to the nation's most massive folly which is situated in Williamson Park on the outskirts of Lancaster. With its huge green dome and majestic appearance it is a prominent landmark, especially when viewed from the nearby M6. It looks like a library, a public building attached to a university perhaps, but the truth is that this fabulous structure, a masterpiece of Edwardian baroque architecture reminiscent of the earlier masterpieces of Wren, Hawksmoor and Vanbrugh serves no useful function whatsoever. This is as good a definition of a folly as you can get!! The building is clad in white Portland stone, but its heart is (metaphorically speaking) made from lino!

James Williamson was the second son of James Williamson senior, who ran an oil cloth and linoleum business in Lancaster. It is the usual story. Born in 1842, James Williamson (Junior) worked all his life in the linoleum business, starting work in his father's shop, and eventually taking full control of the business in 1875. He expanded the firm, became a multi-millionaire in the process, and was responsible for laying linoleum on parlour floors from Dallas to Darwin, becoming known as the Lino King in the process.

Williamson was to Lancaster what Lord Leverhulme was to Bolton - simply its chief employer and greatest philanthropist. Honours were showered on him. Appointed High Sheriff of Lancaster in 1885, he followed this up by serving as Liberal MP for Lancaster from 1886 to 1895. In 1895 he was created a peer of the realm assuming the title Baron Ashton of Ashton, after his country seat near Lancaster. Eventually however, he forsook Lancaster for Lytham St Annes, where he died in 1930 at the age of 88 - an eccentric recluse.

The first Williamson to make his mark upon the Lancaster landscape was James Williamson senior, who began the laying out of Williamson Park in the 1870s. A carriage drive and gravel paths were constructed to provide relief work for laid off operatives during the Cotton Famine. The top of the carriage drive was known as the "Top of Hard Times". A stone seat bearing the inscription "Rev T.R, London 1863" survives from this period. The plan was to include elaborate landscaping with an ornamental lake and an artificial waterfall. It was a formidable undertaking, and Williamson never lived to see his work completed. That task fell to his son - Lord Ashton.

James Williamson junior gave the park to Lancaster Corporation in 1881, and it was formally opened for public use in 1896. In 1904 the Park was improved and Sir John Belcher was commissioned to design a temple, a fountain, a palmhouse and last (but by no means least) the Ashton Memorial.

Ashton's masterpiece was intended to be a Memorial to his first wife, Margaret Gatey, who had died in 1877, but this resolve was diluted somewhat when he remarried in 1880. His second wife, Jessie Hume, died in 1904, and Williamson married yet again in 1909, this time to Florence Maud Whalley, a prosperous widow. In the end, Lord Ashton simply dedicated his memorial to "deceased relatives"!

The Ashton Memorial (or, as it is known locally, the "Jelly Mould") cost £87,000 to build, a fabulous sum in those days. The contractors were Waring and Gillow of Lancaster, better known in their role of cabinet makers. From the very beginning there were problems. Originally conceived as a solid stone structure, rising costs forced the contractors to experiment with cheaper materials - load-bearing brick, steel girders and stone-clad concrete, all of which were to lead to major structural problems in the course of time.

All the same the Memorial is a wondrous constructional cocktail. Its staircases and façades are of Cornish granite, Derbyshire limestone and some 300 tons of finely-worked stone masonry. The monument stands 150 feet high at the summit of the park, and the sense of height is further heightened by the enormous flight of steps on its western side. The interior consists of two domed chambers, one on top of the other, with a host of steps leading out onto various balconies. It is well adorned with frescoes and sculptures. Within the lower dome are four large figure groups painted by George Murray. They represent Commerce, Art, History and Science. These groups are separated by figures representing the four seasons, accompanied by the arms of Lancaster. Sculptured figures, representing similar themes, are found on the exterior of the dome - Science, for example, carries some lab apparatus and a telephone. When nearly completed, the building was opened without ceremony on 24th October 1909.

In 1920 the memorial was reported as being in need of repair. Rain had percolated through the structure and had reacted with impurities in the concrete, causing it to crack. This in turn had exposed the steel joists to the elements, making them corrode. Lord Ashton, though now long fallen out of love with his native town, nevertheless provided funds for the repair of his gigantic white elephant, and after his death his widow continued to do so.

In 1942 the adjacent palm house was damaged by fire and its contents destroyed; and twenty years later, in 1962, the dome of the memorial suffered a similar fate. Attempts were made to preserve the building, but by 1981 it was in such a state of disrepair that it had become structurally unsound and finally had to be closed to the public.

This story however has a happy ending. After an estimate that around £600,000 would be required to restore the memorial an appeal was launched, and with the help of many benefactors the local council was able to undertake a complete restoration of both the memorial and the palm house. Work took place from 1985 to 1987, and in May 1987 the Ashton Memorial was finally re-opened to the public.

Williamson Park today is a delight. Parking is free, and it is a marvellous place to picnic and enjoy the fine views over Lancaster and across Morecambe Bay to the Lakeland mountains. The palmhouse has been restored and is now a butterfly house, and there is an adjacent giftshop and café. The memorial itself is now open to the public, and admission is free to the lower dome, where there is a fine exhibition on the life and times of Lord Ashton. It is also a popular backdrop for outside theatrical productions. Lancaster, it would seem, is beginning to find some worthwhile uses for the Jelly Mould after all.

8: ASHURST'S BEACON AND THE PARBOLD BOTTLE

This pleasant country walk offers fine views over the Douglas Valley from two different vantage points, two interesting monuments, an old hall, a dovecote, and a pleasant stroll along the banks of the Leeds-Liverpool Canal.

Getting there:	Follow A59 Ormskirk to Burscough. Turn right onto the B5239 and pass through Newburgh to Parbold. Turn left into Parbold village and park by the canal, opposite Parbold Mill.
Distance:	6 miles
Map ref:	SD 491 106 Landranger 108
Rating:	Walk ** Follies and General Interest **

Parbold is a summery place, a village of picturesque stone cottages and converted barns. It is possessed of a sleepy rural charm which appears to be quite unaffected by the substantial residential growth which has taken place here in recent years. No doubt this is in part due to its unique geographical location, being situated where the foothills of upland Lancashire finally give way to the coastal plain. To the west, everything is table flat. This is a land of glasshouses, tomatoes and arable fields - Lancashire's "garden".

Eastwards, however, the landscape is quite different. Parbold nestles at the foot of its dominating hill, up which the road winds on its way to Standish and Wigan. The summit of Parbold Hill is a popular viewpoint, with fine views over the Douglas Valley. It is the last gasp of upland Lancashire.

Parbold has a long history. In mediaeval times it was a part of the Barony of Manchester, and was held by the Lathom family of Lathom in the thirteenth century. It was always a farming community, and Parbold's windmill, which stands by the canal at the start of our walk, is evidence of this. The arrival of the canal at Parbold stimulated further developments, both coal and stone

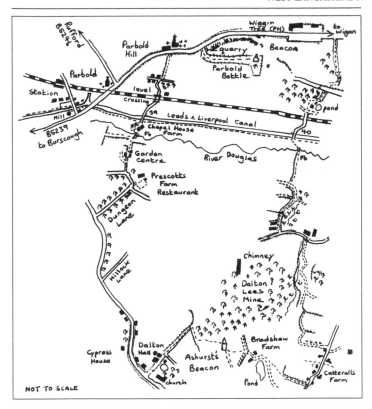

NOT TO SCALE

coming from the surrounding hills for barge shipment, the coal being sent to supply the gasworks in Liverpool.

The mining did little, however, to mar the status of Parbold as a residential area. Towards the end of the last century, Parbold became a summer retreat for wealthy Manchester cotton merchants, and most of their grand houses remain. A new form of residential development has appeared on the canal side, and the canal itself is alive with cruisers and narrowboats.

Our route leaves the village courtesy of the canal towpath. Eventually, after passing over a charming hand-gated level crossing,

Ashurst's Beacon

we reach the main road and plod up Parbold Hill. Just before reaching the popular viewpoint by the Wiggin Tree Inn, we detour round the perimeter fence of the quarry to examine the Parbold Bottle.

The Parbold Bottle, as follies go, is neither massive nor impressive. It is, however, decidedly curious. As its name suggests it is shaped like a bottle, but the shape is more like an eighteenth-century port bottle than a modern receptacle. It is made of the local gritstone, and was erected to com-

memorate the 1832 Reform Bill. This viewpoint is excellent, and just off the beaten track. The coastal plain is spread out below, and there is a lovely view across the Douglas Valley. Two other follies are visible: Ashurst's Beacon on the hillside opposite, and, from the adjacent road, Blackpool Tower can be seen to the north-west. In the foreground are Parbold's two Victorian churches and their sheer grandness of scale testifies to the wealth of Parbold's nineteenth-century residents. Both churches were very much the gifts of influential local families.

From the Parbold Bottle we retrace our steps to the road and continue on to the summit of Parbold Beacon. Across the road, all mod cons are available at the Wiggin Tree, which is highly developed to cope with the influx of local tourists.

From the top of Parbold Hill we descend to the canal once more, skirting quarries and woodlands en route, before finally re-crossing the cut at Bridge 40. We continue onwards, crossing the River Douglas and passing over fields to a lane. Beyond an interesting farmstead with a quaintly dilapidated seventeenth-century frontage and a ball finial made of wood, we start our ascent up the opposite side of the valley. Passing woodlands, we skirt what was formerly the perimeter of the Dalton Mine. From vast underground quarries, thousands of tons of roofing flags were once extracted, but now the entrances to the workings are sealed off and little trace remains of what was once an extensive industry.

Entering a narrow lane near the entrance to the tantalizingly named Bangham Farm our route ascends at last to the summit of Ashurst's Beacon and a truly excellent prospect. Ashurst's Beacon was erected on Ashurst Hill in 1798 by Lord Skelmersdale during the Napoleonic Wars. This was the last time that the beacons were used to warn of imminent danger, beacon sites long out of use being refurbished and manned during this period. Frequently a guard house was constructed for the soldiers manning the beacon, and this may have been the building's original purpose. Today the doors and windows are bricked up, but at least Ashurst's Beacon still retains its pyramidical top (which is more than can be said for neighbouring Billinge Beacon).

An inscription on one side of the structure informs us that it was presented to Wigan Corporation in 1962 by Mrs Florence Meadows in memory of her journalist husband Thomas, who desired that the beacon should be a public beauty spot. Those wishes have been respected with a bonus, for the area has now been developed into a country park. Ashurst's Beacon stands at 570 feet above sea level, and dominates Skelmersdale when viewed from the coastal plain. The view here is superior to that of Parbold Hill, and in addition to Blackpool Tower, the Merseyside coast and the Clwydian hills, Winter Hill and Rivington Pike may also be discerned to the north-east. A fine prospect indeed.

From Ashurst's Beacon we descend the hillside to Dalton. Dalton Hall in 1640 was a "large castellated edifice", but now is rebuilt as a modern house after having been demolished some years ago. Mercifully the destruction was not complete - the original seventeenth-century porch and adjacent dovecote survived. The dovecote is now restored, and the old porch is incorporated into the fabric of the new house. A plaque on the side of the dovecote informs us that "This 17th century Stone Columbarium was restored by the North West Buildings Preservation Trust. 1985". Adjacent to the dovecote is a most incredibly stagnant pond.

From Dalton we proceed (via the exquisitely shady Dungeon Lane) to Prescotts Farm and a footbridge over the River Douglas. Just before turning into Chapel House Farm, a cross surrounded by iron railings appears on the right. The inscription explains all:

Here stood Old Douglas Chapel, for four full centuries loved and thronged by those who worshipped God from all the country round.

EXISTED 1526
REBUILT 1821 DEMOLISHED 1875

The Holy Table, Font and Pulpit are now in
Douglas Parish Church.
This cross, carved from the old threshold stone
was erected July 1906
"Your father's where are they?"

Returning to the canal at Bridge 39, we turn left for Parbold, and the end of our perambulation.

On a sunny summer's afternoon Parbold is a place to linger, to sit back, to relax, feed the ducks and savour the gently lapping waters of the canal. Here there are no wild moors, no seascapes, no wuthering breezes, just a gently attractive and seductively subtle charm.

The Walk

Start at Parbold Mill Bridge (no.37D). Cross the bridge on Mill Lane and turn left onto the canal towpath, passing the Old Mill Farmshop on the right. Pass under the B 5239 (Bridge no.38) and continue onwards to Chapel House Bridge (no.39). Cross the bridge and proceed to a gated level crossing. Pass over the railway and proceed to a junction by houses. Ignore tracks leading off to the left and right and instead search for an elusive stile opposite, slightly to the right.

Parbold Mill

The path leads up the pasture side to enter the busy B5239.

Cross the road and turn right up Parbold Hill, passing the church on the left. Near the summit, recross the road by the entrance to the Landfill site, where a gate warns "Danger Private Property". To the right of this gate, another, smaller gate and stile gives access to a grassy path which winds around the quarry perimeter to the Parbold Bottle.

Retrace your steps back to the B5239 and turn right, along a pathway running alongside the road. This soon reaches an area of parked cars and picnic tables on the summit of Parbold Beacon. Just beyond, turn right down a signed and well surfaced path running down the hillside. This crosses the lower access road to the quarry, then continues down the perimeter of woodland on the edge of a quarry face. The route passes houses and a pond and then crosses the railway before reaching the canal at bridge no.40.

Cross the canal, bearing left to a footbridge over the River Douglas. Follow a marshy track onwards, and on joining a farm road turn left, the farm road leads without complication up the hillside, passing a house with stables to emerge into a tarmac lane.

Turn left along the lane for a short distance, and then, by a fine old seventeenth-century farmhouse turn right through a stile and gate, following a grassy track up the hillside. In the vicinity of the former Dalton Lees Mine the route becomes confusing. Where the track peters out by an old fence, look for a stile in the fence on your left, pass through it, and continue uphill with the fence now on your right. On reaching a farm track, turn left along it, to reach another lane opposite the entrance to Bangham Farm.

Turn right up the steep lane, passing housing and Catterall's Farm on the left. Between the Manor House (on the left) and the entrance to Bradshaw Farm (on the right), follow an overgrown path leading off right between fences. This crosses an open field before joining the track to Bradshaw Farm. Turn right along the track which winds to the left, passing a small lake. Pass through farm buildings to a small gate, beyond which the path leads over open common to Ashurst's Beacon.

From Ashurst's Beacon follow a steep path down the hillside towards the tower of Dalton church. At the bottom of the slope bear right through trees, then left through a stile, following a descending path between fences to farm buildings and the old entrance porch and dovecote of Dalton Hall. Continue onwards along the track, passing the church on the left. On entering the tarmac lane, turn right down the hill, passing various houses en route.

Ignore Hillock Lane on the right but just beyond it bear right down Dungeon Lane. At the junction, bear left, and on the bend turn right down a track signed "Lees Lane Garden Centre". Pass through farm buildings and follow a track towards the river. At the T-junction ignore tracks to the left and right and cross the field to a footbridge over the River Douglas. Cross the pasture to Chapel House Farm, passing the cross on the right.

On regaining the canal at bridge no.39 turn left and follow the canal towpath back to Parbold Mill.

Dalton Hall

9: BILLINGE BEACON

The main attraction of this short and initially unpromising walk is the excellent view over Merseyside to the Welsh mountains. The heavily vandalised Summer House is a fine example of just what should NOT be allowed to happen to our prospect towers and follies.

Getting there:	Take the A571 out of Wigan, passing over the M6. The church is at junction of A571 and B5207. Park in recreation ground by public toilets opposite.
Distance:	2 miles. Easy
Map ref:	Beacon SD 526 015 Landranger 108
Rating:	Walk * Follies and General Interest *

Billinge is the sort of place you would usually pass through on your way elsewhere. This hilltop village, straggling the road between Wigan and St Helens, has the air of an old community whose fortunes, like the pattern of its development, have gone gradually downhill. Despite a nucleus of old buildings opposite the church, Billinge is essentially a redundant pit village lost in the no man's land of the virtually defunct Lancashire coalfield.

Billinge's main feature of interest is its church. The first chapel to serve this hilltop village was constructed in 1534 and was not, it seems, officially consecrated, as there is no trace of any dedication. In 1552 it was visited by the King's Commissioners, who found that the chapel contained little of any value. It was re-furnished, only to be wrecked in the reign of Queen Mary, when the windows were smashed, and the building used as a barn for storing hay. It was not until the eighteenth century that religious interest was rekindled, when James Scarisbricke provided the funds for its reconstruction in 1718. The oak panelling and altar table, along with the fine brass candelabrum date from this period.

Externally the building is oblong with a rounded apse. It has classical Doric columns supporting a long stone roof. The windows

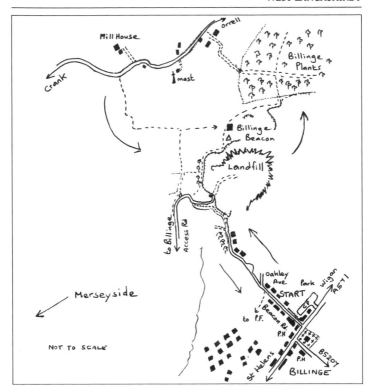

contain some fine blue Victorian glass. Beneath the record board there is a brass plate to James Scarisbricke, dated 1721. On the outside parapet are stone urns, and the building has a fine cupola containing a massive bell. The whole picture is one of eighteenth-century elegance.

Less elegant is the start of our walk. After an uninspiring stroll through a housing estate, we gradually take to a footpath running around the perimeter of an unsightly (and smelly) landfill site. Beyond, a well worn path winds up to the summit of Billinge Beacon, where a triangulation pillar hides behind an unsightly wall and fence on the very edge of the rubbish-filled chasm.

Behind us is the Summer House which originally belonged to

nearby Winstanley Hall. It was also intended as a daymark to shipping. It is a building of gross ugliness - a square concrete floored box completely daubed from top to toe in lurid graffiti. A single doorway gives access to the dark interior. It seems incredible to think that this was once a building of some elegance. The building originally, we are told, had a pyramid roof, which would have made it very like its neighbour, nearby Ashurst's Beacon. Alas, there is little resemblance to it now.

Yet despite its unpromising appearance, Billinge Beacon is a highly popular local resort. It was thronging with people when we visited it, people talking and picnicking, couples courting, even an artist sitting there pastelling the view. People come here for the view, and there is certainly no faulting that! Billinge Beacon looks mainly to the south-west. Liverpool, with its two cathedrals and highly distinctive skyline, is immediately apparent, and beyond, across the Dee, may be seen the mountains of North Wales. Nearer at hand is the industrial sprawl of nearby St Helens, framed in the Cheshire Hills on the far side of the Mersey, and to the left the great bowl of Greater Manchester clearly seen. Westwards is the coastal plain and the dunes leading up to Southport. Were it not for the adjacent landfill and the noise of juveniles on motorbikes, this would be a most pleasant and peaceful spot.

Beyond the beacon things improve a bit. A newly erected kissing gate gives access to Billinge Plants, a fine broadleaved wood happily in the possession of the Woodland Trust. This woodland is reminiscent of the type of woods found frequently in the Yorkshire Coalfield - "bell ground" plantations dotted with the spoil of early mining operations. Here of course, we are in the Lancashire Coalfield so the similarity should not be too surprising.

The rest of the walk is quite pleasant: arable fields, picturesque cottages and a footpath which quickly becomes a fine promenade along a high level contour offering superb views over Merseyside. I have commented on the unsavoury aspects of this walk, but yet the ugliness is only skin deep. When the tip is full it will be landscaped and grassed over. Even now the Summer House could be restored to a semblance of its former glory, and the hilltop developed into a small country park. If the hordes of local picnickers are anything to go by, the demand is most certainly there. All that is lacking is the will and the money. Here is not only a beautifully sited folly, but also one of the finest viewpoints in Lancashire. Will Billinge Beacon be left to the exclusive attentions of the vandals? We must hope not!

The Walk

Start at the car park by the public conveniences in Billinge. Proceed along Beacon Road, passing through a large residential area. Beyond the Old Vicarage, by the landfill site gates, the road narrows to an enclosed path, running alongside the perimeter fence. This path leads into the main site access road. Turn left onto the access road, and follow it a short distance until a path appears on the right, running through a tunnel of bushes alongside the perimeter fence. A short distance up this is joined by another path and proceeds without difficulty to the "folly" on Billinge Beacon.

After enjoying the view continue onwards alongside the fence to a stile at the entrance to Billinge Plants. Proceed through the wood a short distance, then turn left onto a track which runs across your path. This leads to a gate at the edge of the wood, and passes over arable fields to join a lane by cottages. Turn left into the lane, which winds around to the right, passing masts. Just beyond the track to Millhouse, turn left, following a fine high level footpath along the contour. The path bears left, and where it joins a path leading directly back to the Beacon bear right. Continue onwards to the landfill access road. Here turn left and retrace the outward route back to the centre of Billinge.

10: BLACKPOOL TOWER

It is stating the obvious to say that Blackpool contains a most interesting and curious prospect tower. It is in fact, to quote its own advertising, "Britain's Biggest, Boldest, Brightest and Best!" Need I say more?

Map ref:	SD 305 361 Landranger 102
Rating:	Follies and General Interest ***

Blackpool is an old tart - gaudy, loud, brash, tasteless and above all "for hire". Grinning grotesquely she will relieve you of your cares - and your cash! What elemental force, what bizarre yearning can (after you have explored the wild and lonely places of this jewel of English counties) possibly draw the lover of peace and quiet to this seemingly soulless and godforsaken place?

The answer stands exactly 518 feet 9 inches above the flat Fylde countryside. Standing on the lonely summit of Clougha Pike, it beckons from across the marshes of the Wyre. It calls you from Darwen Tower, from Ashurst's Beacon and from distant Hampsfell Hospice across the sands of Morecambe Bay. From Formby Point (in the wake of Ince Blundell) you can see it shimmering in the haze along the endless flat sands, and from lonely Sambo's Grave it seems "nobbut a cock stride away!" From every point of Lancashire, north or south, high or low, one single image captures the imagination and draws it like a beacon. That beacon is Blackpool Tower.

Let's start at the beginning. At the turn of the eighteenth century, Blackpool was nothing more than a few fishermen's huts on the dunes of a lonely coast. Had it not been for the foibles of fashion, it would probably have remained that way, but fashion created Blackpool, and she has remained a dedicated follower ever since.

In the 1740s, Blackpool was "discovered" by some adherents to the then fashionable craze for sea bathing. They waxed lyrical about the health giving properties of the place, and soon others followed in their wake. In consequence, Blackpool gradually began to develop into a popular sea bathing resort. No doubt it would have remained

Blackpool Tower

a small but undistinguished spa town had it not been for one singular development in the 1840s - the coming of the railway.

The railway, a novel and cheap form of transport, brought in ordinary working-class folk in pursuit of a good time. Their tastes were unsophisticated and frequently vulgar, and Blackpool wasted no time in pandering to them. In 1863 the North Pier was officially opened, and in 1868 the forerunner of the Central Pier was erected. By 1870 a promenade had been built, and the Winter Gardens, with its tea rooms, dance floors and opera house, had become a major attraction.

Blackpool Tower was the brainchild of John Bickerstaffe, Mayor of Blackpool and Director of the Blackpool Electric Tramways

Company. It all began in the 1880s with a business trip to Paris, where Bickerstaffe marvelled at the Eiffel Tower which had been constructed for the Great Exhibition. Blackpool, he fancied, would look good with one of those, and on his return he set to work with a will. A Blackpool Tower Company was formed, consisting of five directors - Alderman John Dickins, a former Mayor of Salford, Wilfred Anderton of Preston, Arthur Lawcock of Whitchurch, William Bratby of Hale, Cheshire, and Bickerstaffe himself.

The Tower, designed by Maxwell and Tuke, was constructed on the site of Doctor Cocker's Aquarium and Menagerie.The aquarium was not demolished, but was incorporated into the complex, its turtles (amazingly) being the same ones that stare superciliously down at you today. The foundation stone of the Tower was laid on 25th September 1891. The foundation contract was agreed at £3,000 and the original tender to build the tower was £42,000, a phenomenal sum in those days. (And it was expected that the complex buildings would cost a further £36,000.)

The Tower Ballroom is magnificent and is a grade two listed structure. What the humble workers of Oldham and Rochdale must have thought of such Edwardian magnificence is surely a treat for the imagination. Dance around the Tower Ballroom to the strains of the mighty Wurlitzer Organ, made eternally famous by the great Reginald Dixon, and you are dancing through almost a century of history in the footsteps of departed generations. For all human life is here - love and laughter, sadness and despair, sickness, birth and death. Few places can have the atmosphere of the Tower Ballroom.

The Tower took three years to build. It was officially opened on 14th May 1894, along with its ballroom and circus, and the world came to marvel at this man-made giant standing so high above the flat Fylde countryside.

And a giant it certainly is! Blackpool Tower contains 3,478 tons of steel and 352 tons of cast iron, each of its four huge legs rests on concrete blocks 35 feet square by 12 feet thick. The blocks are reinforced with girders and the whole thing rests on boulder clay. Five million bricks were used in the construction. Maintenance of the "stick" is a constant headache for the twenty riggers, painters and welders whose job it is to preserve the Tower from the wind and the rain. Like the Forth Bridge, the Tower has to be continually repainted. In 1977, to celebrate Queen Elizabeth II's jubilee, it was briefly painted silver. There are four viewing levels on the top of the Tower, accessed by iron newel staircases. The higher up you go, the more nervous you get! There is a fifth (ultra precarious!) level, but this is locked up. Notices threaten dire penalties for those throwing objects over the "side" and rightly so!

Today the Tower reigns supreme in Blackpool, but it was not always so. The nearby Winter Gardens did not take too kindly to this upstart rival that was stealing their trade and resolved to hit back. This they did by constructing a giant Ferris wheel, modelled on the famous one in Vienna. This wheel (designed by the inventor of the vacuum cleaner, Hubert Cecil Booth), was 240 feet high (half the height of the tower!) and had thirty cars around its circumference, each capable of carrying thirty passengers. The so-called "Battle of the Giants" began in 1896, when the big wheel began turning, but ultimately it was the Winter Gardens who were the losers. The trouble with a giant Ferris wheel is its slow speed and the phenomenal amount of time it takes to load it with passengers. The Blackpool wheel travelled at a half a mile per hour, which made it slow, time-consuming and generally boring. Ultimately it could not compete with the attractions of the tower and in 1928 it was finally dismantled, the cars being sold off at £13 apiece. Eventually the Blackpool Tower Company purchased the Winter Gardens itself, and the spirit of competition was finally laid low.

From Blackpool Tower you return to the bright lights of the Golden Mile. Walking on the prom after dark you stand on the borderline between two worlds, on one side of you the illuminations, the noise, the clamour, the glitz, and on the other darkness and silence - save for the gentle lapping of the sea below the beach steps. It is in a sense, a microcosm of the two Lancashires - the one made by man and the other by nature. As in the Tower Ballroom - All Life is here!

11: JUBILEE TOWER, QUERNMORE AND CLOUGHA PIKE

Sombre, lonely moors, and fabulously extensive views are the hallmark of this invigorating tramp in the Bowland Fells, starting and finishing at the castellated Jubilee Tower with its fine views over nearby Lancaster.

Getting there:	Take the Trough of Bowland road out of Lancaster, passing under the M6. Beyond Quernmore and Brow Top Farm the road takes to the open fell below Clougha Pike. The Jubilee Tower is quite unmistakable. Park in the car park opposite.
Distance:	8 miles
Map ref:	SD 542 573 Landranger 102
Rating:	Walk *** Follies and General Interest **

Most of the follies visited in this book have to be walked to. This particular walk, however, is exceptional in that our object is located at the start of the walk. The Jubilee Tower stands above Quernmore, beside the fell road which leads from Lancaster through the Trough of Bowland to Dunsop Bridge. There is a car park adjacent - a popular resort for motorists who like to sit in their cars and enjoy the extensive views. Few bother to lace up their boots and take to the open fell. Alas, they don't realise what they are missing.

The Jubilee Tower is basically a castellated viewing platform served by an exterior stone staircase. It appears to be solid, there being no bricked up doors or windows at ground level to suggest the former presence of a lower chamber. The tower was largely the work of a Mr Harrison, a native of Quernmore, and an inscribed tablet informs us that:

> THIS TOWER
> WAS ERECTED BY
> JAMES HARRISON

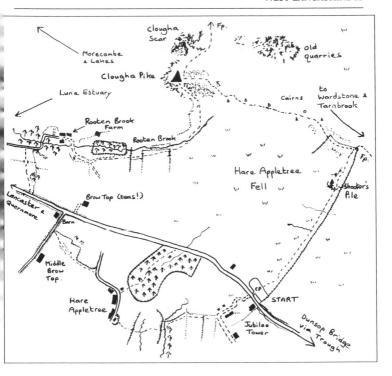

OF HARE APPLETREE
IN COMMEMORATION OF THE
JUBILEE OF HER MAJESTY
QUEEN VICTORIA
ANNO DOMINI 1887

Harrison, who had made his fortune as a Liverpool shipbuilder, employed a local mason named Gifford (who had also worked on Quernmore Church and Chapel) to do most of the work on the tower. Gifford did his work well - his sturdy structure was built to withstand the cruel wind and the driving rain, hail and snow that so frequently belabour these bleak uplands during the winter months. So far, it has responded well to this challenge.

The tower has had a chequered history. It was originally in

private ownership but was given to Lancashire County Council in 1973 by Mr Adam Leigh of Hare Appletree. The council at the same time began work on the present car park, and spent a considerable amount on developing the surrounding area. By 1977, however, the Lancaster Civic Society was reporting that the tower seemed to be in a poor condition, despite the council having resurfaced the viewing platform and repointed most of the stonework. Shortly afterwards the handrail was repaired, and the tower fully restored. The wind and the rain still buffet this battered structure, but with the adjacent car park and the constant influx of summer visitors, its future (unlike many such buildings) seems assured.

The tower stands at 940 feet above sea level, and on a clear day the view is phenomenal, ranging from the Fylde coast to the Lake District. You might be forgiven for thinking this the finest view in Lancashire, but you would be wrong, for that view is yet to come - on the summit of Clougha Pike.

From the car park a path leads up onto Hare Appletree Fell. This is an ancient landscape and, not surprisingly, there are evidences of ancient people. When the car park was constructed in 1973, a seventh-century burial was uncovered by a mechanical excavator. The grave contained a coffin which had been made from a hollowed-out tree trunk. Of the corpse only the hair and fingernails remained, but the cloth shroud in which it had been wrapped was excellently preserved, and is in fact one of the largest pieces of Dark Age cloth ever found in Britain. The remains are now on display in the Lancaster City Museum.

A short distance up the moor and an area of peat channel reveals further evidences of ages past. Embedded in the peat, in a state of perfect preservation, are the branches and roots of birch trees that once clothed this bleak fellside. These are not fossils - the wood has been perfectly preserved and bears the appearance of being felled only recently, but its provenance rules out any such possibility. Perhaps the log in which our unknown dark age warrior was buried in the seventh century came from the same woodlands as these tantalising half buried morsels, which still retain their original bark.

Hare Appletree Fell, along with much of the bleak landscape around Clougha Pike, is designated an Access Area - a place where the public can wander freely in certain "controlled sectors". The

Jubilee Tower, Quernmore

Bowland Fells are the largest expanse of privately-owned hill country in England, and, perhaps more than anywhere else, typify the ongoing struggle between land-owning mediaevalism on the one hand and public recreational access to open country on the other. The Clougha Access Area consists of 1,717 acres of open moorland, which sounds impressive until you realise the extent of the moorlands you are not allowed to enter.

The ascent of the moor along the boundary fence to the cairn at Shooters Pike is a surprisingly long and arduous one. It is also, until the jumble of boulders is reached near the top, rather wet and muddy. According to the map we are very near the "Castle of Cold Comfort" but there is no building in view. A ladder stile at a junction of fences announces the start of the "access corridor" which leads around the moorland ridges to Gritfell, Wardstone and Tarnbrook.

Our route remains in the Access Area and proceeds round to the summit of Clougha Pike, a fine and surprisingly lengthy moorland walk. Clougha Pike is, quite literally, the high point of our walk. The summit is unmistakable with its cairn, trig point and rough stone wind shelter. Around it there is much disturbed ground, the remains of long disused quarries. Long, long ago millstones were made here, parts of the workings dating back to Roman times and beyond, when stone querns, those tiny manually operated forerunners of the modern flour mill, were exported from here in large numbers. Querns were made for domestic use, and the Romans industrialised the process, opening up large quarries, their location being evidenced in the distribution of place names - Whernside, Quernhow and, of course Quernmore.

The name Clougha Pike is supposedly of Old English origin and means "projecting ridge", a not particularly surprising observation, for that is exactly what it is! However, there are other interpretations. It has also been suggested that the name means "Great Rock", being derived from the old Irish "Clogha", or "abundance of showers" from the Celtic "Glagwog".

Considering its position it should come as no surprise to find that beacons have been lit on the pike, although it does not seem to have been part of the traditional beacon system which was used in times of national emergency. The last beacon to be lit here was to celebrate VE day, and on the occasion of Queen Victoria's Jubilee a beacon was lit by the same Mr Harrison who built the Jubilee Tower, the undertaking of this task involving a hazardous ascent to the summit in a pony and trap.

The view from Clougha Pike, if it is clear, quite literally takes the breath away. Here on this wind blown eminence we are standing on the roof of Lancashire. The actual height is about 1,500 feet above sea level. Pendle at 1,831 feet is higher, but even that great eminence cannot compete with the amazing prospect here! As at the Jubilee Tower, the Fylde coast is in full view, Blackpool Tower being particularly noticeable in the south-west. Fleetwood and the Wyre Estuary can be plainly seen, along with the estuary of the Lune, a silvery swaithe stretching down to the sea at Sunderland Point. The massive square box to the right is the nuclear power station at Heysham. In the foreground is Lancaster, with its grim castle, and the green dome of The Ashton Memorial. Beyond lie the sands of Morecambe Bay, and a spectacular view across to Grange and the mountains of the Lake District! This prospect is also seen from the Jubilee Tower, but here at Clougha Pike we have the additional bonus of open views to the north and east. To the north we can scan the Lune Valley, and make out the "Crook of Lune". Beyond, the river winds up to Kirkby Lonsdale and eventually the Howgill Fells, where it rises. Towards Morecambe Bay, Carnforth, Warton Crag, Jenny Brown's Point and Silverdale are in view, while to the east the western edges of the Yorkshire Dales, dominated by the flat summit of Ingleborough, pop up behind the sombre Bowlands on our near horizon. There is much, much more. All of northern Lancashire is laid out for you to see, and in this lonely spot you will, more likely than not, have it all to yourself.

To Quernmore it is downhill all the way. After descending the rocky, scree strewn slopes, we follow Rowton Brook down to the intake level, eventually joining the fell road just above Quernmore. Rowten (or Rooten) Brook has some interesting stories attached to it. One tale concerns Jenette Cragg, who lived at Rooten Brook Farm in the seventeenth century. Her son-in-law, John Kelsall, was a Quaker, who was much persecuted for his faith. He died in 1687 en route for the West Indies, whither he had been banished. His wife died shortly afterwards, leaving two orphaned boys. Their grandmother, Jenette, when she heard of their plight, promptly mounted her pony and rode to London to find her grandchildren - a journey of around 230 miles, no mean achievement in those days. She eventually returned to Rooten Brook Farm, carrying the orphans in her panniers. She died here in 1699.

Rowton Brook in the eighteenth century was the hub of a local hat making industry. Billycock hats and sea caps were made here for export, mainly for wear by slaves and convicts. In the eighteenth century the area was also notorious as being a repository for contraband brandy brought in from Glasson Dock. The remoteness of the area, along with its proximity to the lonely road leading through the Trough of Bowland into Yorkshire, made it an ideal location for these illicit activities.

Our walk does not visit Quernmore, but a diversion may be made. Quernmore's jewel is its church, St Peter's, a decorated fourteenth-century style structure which was built in 1860. Much of the stone was quarried on Clougha, and the east window consists of stained glass depicting the Nativity, Crucifixion and Resurrection, all of which was salvaged from the wreck of the *Fairy Vision* which was lost in fog near the mouth of the River Rhône. The original window, it seems, was made in Lancaster and was intended for export to France, but the ship sank so consequently a new set of windows were made, and the order delivered. Then, amazingly, the original glass was salvaged and promptly shipped back here to Quernmore. So somewhere in France there must still be a set of matching windows.

Quernmore (pronounced "Kworma") has an ancient history. In 1774 a Roman kiln was discovered in the area along with tiles, bricks and pottery ware dating from about AD 204. Slate was quarried in the area, and there are numerous old trackways. The Pendle witches passed this way en route for Lancaster Castle, and many other travellers have since followed in their wake. Today it is bypassed by the M6 and those Sunday drivers heading for Lancaster from the Trough of Bowland.

Leaving the road by a most curious-looking barn, our route takes to the fields once more, passing through Hare Appletree. Beyond, after a confusing route we join the farm road which leads up past Westfield House back to the Jubilee Tower and the end of our journey. If you have the time (and the energy) you could drive onwards towards Lancaster to take a look at The Ashton Memorial. More likely than not, though, you will break out the flask and sandwiches, put your feet up in the car and enjoy that magnificent view!

The Walk

Start at the Jubilee Tower car park. Follow a long (and at times boggy) path up the hillside alongside the access area boundary fence to Shooter's Pile, a cairn on the skyline. Cross rocky ground to a ladder stile at the fence corner. Do not pass over the stile, instead bear left alongside the fence to a second stile, beyond which a cairned and sometimes stony path proceeds over open moorland to a ladder stile and thence to the triangulation pillar and cairn on the summit of Clougha Pike.

From the Pike bear steeply left down the side of the hill, then bear right, skirting a boggy area before crossing Rowton Brook.

Worsley Delph
and (inset) The Fountain

Parbold Hill and
(inset) the Parbold Bottle

Proceed downhill with the brook on the right, passing through three gateways before recrossing the stream, at Rooten Brook Farm.

Pass farm buildings, following the farm road down the hillside. Bearing left, it recrosses the stream above a wooded glen before being joined by another track by a cattle-grid. Continue onwards a short distance then turn left, passing over two pastures along an indistinct path, before entering the Quernmore Road, just above a converted barn.

Turn left up the road a short way, then, just before reaching Brow Top, turn right along a farm road passing behind an odd looking, ruined barn. Take the first stile on the left, crossing the field diagonally along the line of a shallow gully. Over the brow the route follows a fence before joining the farm road to Hare Appletree House. Pass the house on the right and descend through farm buildings to a gate and a cow wallow.

The right of way is not at all apparent! Bear right up the pasture beyond to a rusty iron ladder stile over a fence. Beyond, cross over rough, wet ground to a fence stile by a brook, at the end of a line of trees. Cross the brook and bear left, following the fence and stream uphill to a wall stile adjacent to the access area. Beyond the stile follow the wallside via a fence stile and boulders to a farm road. Turn left, passing Westfield House on the right before rejoining the Quernmore Road by the Jubilee Tower.

12: SILVERDALE PEPPERPOT AND ARNSIDE TOWER

On this fine walk we sample a jubilee "Pepperpot" and the ruins of a mediaeval pele tower, but the real attraction is the woodlands, which are extensive, original and incredibly beautiful.

Getting there:	From the M6 exit 35, turn left down the A6 to Carnforth. At the lights in the centre of Carnforth turn right, passing the railway station on the road to Warton. At Warton turn left, following the road to Crag Foot and Silverdale Station. At the next junction bear left to the National Trust car park at the bottom of Eaves Wood.
Distance:	5 miles
Map ref:	SD 471 759 Landranger 97
Rating:	Walk *** Follies and General Interest **

The area between Arnside and Silverdale on the eastern edge of Morecambe Bay is a veritable walker's paradise. Topographically speaking, the area is a rocky limestone peninsula, for the most part heavily wooded. Formerly it was surrounded by the sands of Morecambe Bay on the one side and by marshes and mosses on the other, with frequent incursions by the sea up the connecting valleys. Bypassed by the traditional "oversands" route from Lancaster, the Arnside/Silverdale area long remained wild and remote, an unspoilt rural backwater quite unknown to the world before being "discovered" by the novelist Mrs Gaskell in the last century. Mrs Gaskell lived for long periods at Lindeth Tower (see Appendix) and she was one of the first people to be sold on the beauties of the area. Many others have followed in her wake.

Eaves Wood belongs to the National Trust, who acquired it in sections over a number of years. This walk is unique in our book in that almost all of it is in woodland, so much so in fact that sometimes you can't see the wood for the trees, and the multiplicity of nature trails and footpaths can make it very easy to get lost. The woodland

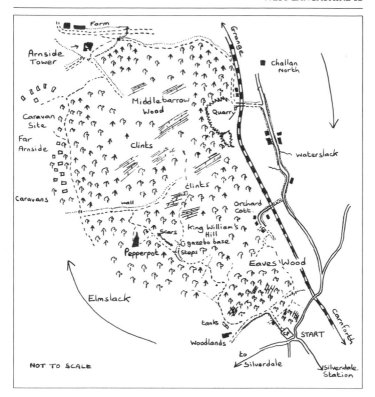

NOT TO SCALE

seclusion is complete and unbroken, and you have to find your way around this leafy maze with care.

Eaves Wood, like its cousin Eggerslack Wood across the sands at Grange, is a wood characterised by limestone scars and pavements, with their associated clints and grykes. As one familiar with the windswept and open limestone country of the Dales I find this heavily-wooded landscape highly unusual, though no doubt much of that area would once have looked much like this, for the Dales landscape is the man-made product of centuries of deforestation by farmers.

Here at Eaves Wood the whole hillside consists largely of

99

ancient and undisturbed woodlands. The bare limestone with its thin soil is home to numerous yew trees, while deeper soils support oak and lime trees. There is also ash, beech, birch, hazel, larch, pine, hawthorn and holly (not to mention areas of grass and heather). The limestone is also of interest, though after heavy rain its smooth pavements can become a slimy, mossy slither for the unwary. In wet weather you should proceed with care.

From the car park our walk passes behind Woodlands, the former residence of Mr Dickins (who donated much of his land to the National Trust in 1929 and on his death in 1949) passing close by the water tanks which originally supplied the house and which were fed from a spring higher up the hillside. A further reminder of the original ownership of the woods appears higher up the hill, when we encounter the stone kerbs and steps which lead to the summit of King William's Hill. Here we can still make out the hexagonal foundations of Mr Dickins' Gazebo, unfortunately well past being saved by the present interest in folly preservation. It was reputedly erected around 1830 in honour of the accession of William IV, after whom the hill was presumably named.

Descending the steps back to the main path, we very quickly reach the summit of Castlebarrow and our chief objective - The Pepperpot. The summit of Castlebarrow stands at over 250 feet above sea level, but being largely backed by dense woodland its only real prospect is to the south-east, where we have a bird's eye view over Silverdale, which lies immediately below us. Further afield however there are other treats. If the weather is really clear, The Ashton Memorial and Blackpool Tower should also be in view, along with the great "box" of Heysham Power Station and the distant summit of Clougha Pike. Looking towards Yorkshire the view is dominated by the table-topped summit of distant Ingleborough, and last, but by no means least, there is the southern part of Morecambe Bay, glittering in the sunshine.

The Pepperpot (originally known as the Pepperbox) is a circular roughstone tower, about twenty feet high with a conical roof. It was built at the instigation of the Hebden family, who then owned Castlebarrow, the builder being a local man by the name of Mr Bowskill. Its purpose (your average folly builder's excuse) was to commemorate the golden jubilee of Queen Victoria in 1887.

The Pepperpot, Silverdale

Apparently there was once a plaque telling the story of the monument, but this fell prey to vandals long ago and was never replaced. During the Great War, soldiers were billeted at nearby Bleasdale House, a Red Cross hospital, and it is said that they planned to build a "Salt Cellar" to keep the Pepperpot company, though nothing was ever done. In 1977 the idea was mooted again, this time the silver jubilee of Queen Elizabeth II being the preferred excuse, but nothing materialised, and we must live in hope of any future efforts.

From Castlebarrow our route, frequented by walkers, caravanners, and rough-spoken men with dogs, deerstalkers and uncovered shotguns, proceeds towards the caravan site.

Proceeding around the caravan site we eventually descend to Arnside Tower. This picturesque ruin, standing on the saddle of land between Castlebarrow and nearby Arnside Knott with its steep forbidding screes (locally called "shilla") has a commanding, dominating presence that was no doubt intentional. Arnside Tower was a defensive structure, and this is reflected in the cunning way in which it was sited, with sea on one side and flat marshes on the other. It seems possible that at one time it could have had the sea on both sides, which would have made it well-nigh unassailable! It was built by the De Broughton family around 1340, and was damaged by fire in 1602. It was restored and survived intact until the end of the seventeenth century, after which it began its steady deterioration. In 1815 it was sold to Daniel Wilson of Dallam, and in 1884 a great storm felled one corner of it. Today it is little more than a shell, although it still retains its fireplaces and sections of newel staircases.

A pele tower was not a great castle or garrison filled with soldiers. It was essentially a home - a tower house which could, if required, be quickly transformed to withstand a sudden attack. Arnside Tower, along with its neighbours at Hazelslack, Borwick, Beetham, Levens, Sizergh and Wraysholme across the sands (see Kirkhead Tower walk), were all built with one purpose in mind - protection from the Scots. Throughout the Middle Ages the Scots were a perpetual threat to the area, frequently invading, killing and looting.

Arnside Tower was unusual in that it had four storeys (most peles had three). The ground floor contained store rooms and a dairy, while steps led up to the entrance, which was on the first floor. Fireplaces and garde robes (latrines) were built into the thickness of the wall. In its heyday a wooden stockade would have been built on the hillside around the tower. This was known as the "Barmkin", and was an enclosure-cum-refuge for cattle and stock.

From Arnside Tower we proceed to the railway and the crossing at Silverdale (Middlebarrow) Quarry. The quarry is owned by Arc and supplies crushed limestone for tarmac, aggregates and agricultural lime. This quarry is the only eyesore on a walk that is otherwise delightful. The limestone has been sliced out of the hillside like the icing on a cake, and the bare cliffs, crowned by the trees of Middlebarrow Woods strike a sombre note. Short of filling the whole cavity with rubbish, how can this deep scar on the landscape ever hope to be removed from view? It is too late. The damage has been done and the scars run deep, the red iron deposits in the white limestone weeping like some geological wound.

Beyond the peaceful grey cottages at Waterslack, we recross the railway and briefly take to the woods once more before turning back down to the car park. The walk has not been an arduous one, and there should be ample time to drive into Silverdale, scout out Arnside Knott for a future ramble or explore the delights of Jenny Brown's Point. This rocky, tree-clad headland will beckon you to explore again, for Silverdale, as I said at the beginning, is a walker's paradise.

The Walk

Start at Eaves Wood car park. Pass through the gate and proceed through the woods, ignoring a path leading off to the right. At the next (T) junction bear left (the same way as the wall), following a well defined footpath along the bottom of the wood. At the fork take the right hand path, passing behind Woodlands and noting old water supply tanks on the left. Just beyond, take the next right, ascending a short distance before turning abruptly left again, following a path which leads past a stone slab seat. Ascend to the right once more, passing through a shattered wall to join another path near a second slab seat. Turn left, passing limestone clints to reach a pathway curb edged with stones and ascending steps to a small gateway in the wall. Detour briefly up the rest of the steps to examine the remains of the Gazebo on King William's Hill. Retrace your steps to the wall gate, and continue onwards, passing low scars on the right. Just beyond, a path leads off left to the Pepperpot on the summit of Castlebarrow.

Return to the main path and continue onwards, winding right to join another path by a wall. Turn left and descend steeply, passing through a wall stile to meet the main footpath to Arnside Tower on the edge of the caravan site. Turn right, pass through a stile, and follow a well gravelled path, with caravans in the trees on the left. At the junction take the right hand fork and follow the path around the base of the hillside to meet another path at an area of open ground, where the steep slopes of Arnside Knott come into view.

Follow this path around to the right, and on reaching the wall bear left, downhill, following the wallside to a ladder stile and the ruins of Arnside Tower.

From Arnside Tower descend the pasture behind the farm to where a (very!) tight stile in the wall on the right gives access to a long, straight path which leads along the bottom of the wood to meet up with the railway crossing at Middlebarrow Quarry. Cross the railway and follow the metalled lane round to Waterslack. Just beyond Waterslack Cottage, a footpath leads off to the right, back over the railway. Recross the railway, and follow the farm track round to the left, passing Orchard Cottage and Eaves Lee Barn. Just beyond Eaves Lee Barn, a footpath (signed "National Trust") leads off to the right, back into the woods. Proceed along this path and pass through a wall stile. Just beyond, ignore the first path leading off to the left and instead take the second left, just before reaching a gate and a small stone shed. This is the outward route and re-enters the car park within a few yards.

Lancashire (Oversands)

13: FINSTHWAITE TOWER

This rough grey-walled tower is literally the "high point" of a steep, predominantly woodland walk starting near the outlet of Lake Windermere. It features a preserved railway, a pleasant village and some fine views of the southern Lake District.

Getting there:	From the M6 junction 36, follow the A591 towards Kendal. Near Sedgwick, turn off onto the Barrow Road (A590) and follow it to Newby Bridge. Park behind the hotel or beside the road leading out to Finsthwaite, just beyond the railway bridge.
Distance:	5 miles
Map ref:	SD 369 865 Landranger 97
Rating:	Walk ** Follies and General Interest *

At Newby Bridge we are actually in the Lake District. Other walks in this book flirt with it, but here, at the outfall of Lake Windermere, we are actually in Lakeland proper. This should come as no surprise, for Coniston and Hawkshead once belonged to Lancashire.

Newby Bridge is where Lake Windermere becomes the River Leven, a lively, rushing river soon fated to be lost in the creeks of Morecambe Bay. At its heart is the old five-arched bridge itself and the adjacent Swan Hotel, which American novelist Nathaniel Hawthorne described in glowing terms when he visited it in 1855. The original bridge over the Leven was a wooden one, which in 1651 was found to be "in great decay", a petition being sent by local worthies to the Bench of Justices in Lancaster appealing for a stone bridge - estimated cost £90.

Newby Bridge's other attraction is the Lakeside and

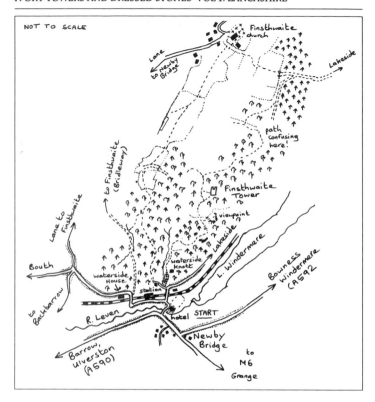

Haverthwaite Railway, the preserved remnant of a railway line which once connected the steamships of Barrow with the steamships of Windermere. Today only three and a half miles of track and three stations remain, but the line still connects with the Windermere Iron Steamship Company's summer ferries up the Lake to Bowness.

Our walk to Finsthwaite Tower begins beyond the railway bridge. I followed the route described in Baddeley's guide to the Lake District, and the directions still hold good. Finsthwaite Tower stands at 400 feet upon the summit of a steep and thickly-wooded bluff, with fine views up Lake Windermere - or so Baddeley's description leads us to believe. In reality, the steep slog up from

Newby Bridge rewards us with a grey tower completely lost in dense woodland. No doubt there is an excellent view from the top of the tower, the only trouble is that it is little more than a shell and the door is walled up. A fine prospect may be enjoyed from a rocky outcrop a bit lower down the slope, but otherwise the hillside is so thickly cloaked with woods that views in any direction are completely shut out.

What they deny you in views, the woodlands hereabouts make up for in quality, comprising mainly of birches, beeches and Scots pines. The beeches have been heavily coppiced, and this gives the wood an untidy, jungle-like quality. The wood is looked after by the Lake District Society for the Protection of Birds. There are, I am informed, deer hereabouts, which does suggest that perhaps Finsthwaite Tower is not subject to frequent human visitation. On the woodland floor, boletes are in evidence, along with numerous examples of the usually uncommon stinkhorn. This marvellously clever fungus has a fruiting body which gives off an offensive stink of rotting carrion, attracting flies in great numbers which settle on the fungus and carry off its spores on their feet.

Finsthwaite Tower (formerly known as the Pennington Lodge Tower) was built by James King of Finsthwaite House in 1799. Its inscription (in the South facing wall) informs us that it was:

ERECTED
To Honor The
Officers, Seamen and marines
Of The
ROYAL NAVY
Whose Matchle∫s Conduct, and
irresistible valour, decisively defeated
the fleets of France, Spain, and Holland
and preserved and protected
LIBERTY AND COMMERCE
1799

The victories referred to were at St Vincent, Camperdown and The Nile in 1797, which was known as the "year of victories". The tower was obviously intended to be a viewpoint, and it is sad that it no longer fulfills this function.

Finsthwaite Tower

From the tower we follow a potentially confusing path, which eventually leaves the woods and takes us across pastures to the charming village of Finsthwaite. Finsthwaite had a church in 1724, but the present church is Victorian, its rugged solidity making it the winner of a competition for the best "small church in a mountain area". In the churchyard is buried Clementina Johannes Sobieska Douglas, a lady with a curious name and a

potentially curious history, reputedly a daughter of the ill-fated Young Pretender, Bonnie Prince Charlie. Here, no doubt, is an interesting tale - assuming the story is true.

From Finsthwaite we follow a footpath which leads over pastures back to Newby Bridge, with fine Lakeland views behind us. After entering the woods, we cut off to the right to join the bridleway which leads down to the Finsthwaite lane, entering it between Waterside House and the railway. There should be time for a ride on a train or a boat, or simply a pint in Newby Bridge. Whatever the case, as you watch the waters of the Leven swirling over the great weir at the outfall of England's largest lake, you will feel the satisfaction of having completed an enjoyable walk - and all of it in Lancashire, whatever the Boundaries Commission might say!

The Walk

Start from Newby Bridge. On the northern side of the railway bridge turn left, onto a track. A few yards along, turn right, onto a path signed Finsthwaite Tower. Ascend steps between fences, passing Waterside Knott on the right. The path ascends with the stream on the left before eventually winding steeply off to the right towards rocks.

Pass through a rocky area and ascend a few steps to arrive at a junction of paths. Take the left-hand path, leading upwards through a shattered wall. (The right-hand path leads to a rocky knoll with fine views.) Ascend through bracken, as Finsthwaite Tower appears on the right, just off the main path and almost hidden by trees.

After inspecting the tower, return to the main path and continue onwards, descending to a junction of paths. Take the right hand path, and bear right then left down the hillside, passing over a fallen tree. At a second fallen tree, bear sharply left, to avoid losing the path, and then at the next junction bear right through a wall gap and descend by conifers to the Finsthwaite Track. Turn left to a seat and gate, then proceed over pastures to Finsthwaite.

At Finsthwaite church pass through a stile (on the left) into pastures, following a footpath signed Newby Bridge. After three stiles enter woodland, and upon reaching a waymarked post take the right hand path which soon joins the Finsthwaite Bridleway near a wall. Turn left onto the bridleway and descend to the Finsthwaite Road by Waterside House. Turn left over the railway then left again to Newby Bridge, with the railway halt and fine views of the river to be encountered en route.

14: HAMPSFELL HOSPICE AND LINDALE

England's warmest resort, fine woodlands, limestone scenery, views to the Lake District and Morecambe Bay, a curious prospect tower, and a positively bizarre cast-iron monument to an "iron mad" industrialist, are the attractions of this excellent and very popular walk high above the sands of Morecambe Bay.

Getting there:	A590-B5277 to Grange Over Sands. Grange is also easily reached by rail.
Distance:	9 miles
Map refs:	Grange station SD 412 782, Hampsfell Hospice SD 399 794 Landranger 97
Rating:	Walk *** Follies and General Interest **

As a seaside resort, Grange is something of a disappointment. True, it has a prom with the traditional iron railings and seats, but sandwiched as it is between the railway line and the mudflats of Morecambe Bay it hardly competes with Blackpool. Grange's attractions lie more in the realms of its mild climate, ornamental lakes and gardens, fine hotels and pleasant woodland walks, the latter being particularly extensive.

Grange-over-Sands does not lie beside Morecambe Bay, rather it perches over it. Grange's hinterland is limestone, steep and rocky, and from the centre of Grange to the summit of the fells is but a short, sweet and decidedly steep ascent through a landscape of sylvan woodlands and limestone pavements. These same fells form a perfect windbreak to the north, and contribute, along with warm air carried here under the influence of the Gulf Stream, to the exceptionally mild climate which Grange enjoys.

Grange itself was largely created by the arrival of the Ulverston and Lancaster Railway in 1857, which brought an influx of gentry to the area, attracted by the mild and charming climate. Prior to this it was little more than a few whitewashed fishermen's cottages. As this formerly isolated community began to develop into a resort it acquired the suffix "-over-Sands", along with the fine Victorian

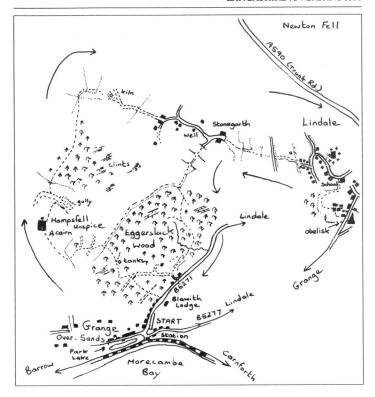

villas, hydropathic establishments, churches and convalescent homes which began to mushroom all over the area.

These were followed by the construction of Grange's fine promenade, wildfowl pond and ornamental gardens, the gardens and rockeries themselves being cunningly designed to screen off the adjacent railway line. Grange's fine clocktower, which stands by St Paul's Church, was built in 1913. It has a peculiarly Germanic character and seems somehow out of place in sedately English Grange.

Our walk starts and finishes on Windermere Road, which leads off from the main road through Grange between the railway station and the wildfowl pond. You should be able to park along Windermere Road. A short distance along the road, we turn into Eggerslack Wood and our walk begins in earnest.

Eggerslack Wood contains many paths and nature trails, and in character is very similar to the woodlands encountered over at Silverdale on the walk to the Pepperpot. This is hardly surprising, as these landscapes are only separated by the Kent Channel and geologically have much the same origins. Eggerslack Wood was originally managed for charcoal burning and the making of baskets and hurdles, but this work declined in the interwar years. The remains of coppicing, however, may still be seen in the clusters of stems growing out of single stumps. The woods consist predominantly of birch, ash, sycamore, oak and hazel, with a sprinkling of beech, larch and wild cherry. The flora is what you would expect in such a fine woodland, and there is much to interest the naturalist. Badgers, foxes and red squirrels occur, along with the occasional roe deer. Eggerslack Wood is a place worthy of detailed exploration.

But not today - for we are here in search of follies. After a long ascent we come out onto the open fell, an area of scrub, limestone pavements and drystone walls, and after an initially confusing tramp up the fellside we suddenly come in sight of our main objective, the squat, square prospect tower of Hampsfell Hospice.

Hampsfell Hospice was built by George Remington, who was Vicar of Cartmel between 1835 and 1854. It was constructed primarily as a viewing platform and shelter for wanderers over the fell. It is essentially a "one up - one down" sort of structure, surrounded by a chain fence on stone blocks. The lower storey contains seats and a fireplace, while the flat roof, reached by precarious stone stairs up the side of the building, forms an admirable lookout platform from which to take in the extensive views ranging from Lancaster to Lakeland. The hospice stands at 727 feet above sea level, and on the roof is a marvellously ingenious and ponderous direction indicator, originally built by a retired railwayman simply for the pleasure of doing it.

The view of course is superb, taking in the Lakeland mountain skyline, the Howgill Fells, the Pennines and Ingleborough, and the Bowland Fells behind Lancaster. Clougha Pike is in view, as is The

Hampsfell Hospice

Ashton Memorial, and nearer at hand the Hoad Monument may be seen to the west, along with Walney and Piel Islands. To the east stands Arnside Knott, between Arnside and Silverdale, and southwards lies Heysham Power Station, beyond which (hopefully) we can see the top of Blackpool Tower. Immediately below us the grey Kirkhead Tower stands on its knoll behind Humphrey Head, and on exceptional days, Snowdon and the Isle of Man should be visible!

Around the walls in the room below are a series of painted boards. They are curious in the extreme and surprisingly unvandalised, though one suspects few visitors take the trouble to read them. This is sad, because more than anything else these hopelessly romantic verses give a marvellous insight into the eccentric character of the kindly clergyman who built the hospice - George Remington:

THE HOSPICE OF HAMPSFELL

THIS HOSPICE HAS AN OPEN DOOR,
ALIKE TO WELCOME RICH AND POOR;
A ROOMY SEAT FOR YOUNG AND OLD
WHERE THEY MAY SCREEN THEM FROM THE COLD

THREE WINDOWS THAT COMMAND A VIEW.
TO NORTH, TO WEST AND SOUTHWARD TOO;
A FLIGHT OF STEPS REQUIRETH CARE,
THE ROOF WILL SHOW A PROSPECT RARE:

MOUNTAIN AND VALE YOU THENCE SURVEY,
THE WINDING STREAMS AND NOBLE BAY:
THE SUN AT NOON THE SHADOW HIDES,
ALONG THE EAST AND WESTERN SIDES.

A LENGTHENED CHAIN HOLDS GUARD ROUND,
TO KEEP THE CATTLE FROM THE GROUND;
KIND READER FREELY TAKE YOUR PLEASURE,
BUT DO NO MISCHIEF TO MY TREASURE:

THE ANSWER

AND IF THE RICH AND POOR SHOULD MEET
I TRUST THEY WILL EACH OTHER GREET,
AND RICH AND POOR AND YOUNG AND OLD
TOGETHER SCREEN THEM FROM THE COLD:

AND AS THE WINDOWS ARE NOT GLASS'D
WE'LL MIND TO LEAVE THE SHUTTERS FAST,
THE "FLIGHT OF STEPS REQUIRETH CARE"
THEN WHY NOT HAVE A HANDRAIL THERE;
THAT FEEBLE OLD AND TIMID FAIR
MAY MOUNT AND VIEW THE PROSPECT RARE:

THE BLUE AND LOFTY MOUNTAIN'S SIDES
THE NOBLE BAY AND STEALTHY TIDES,

THAT TREACHEROUS CREEP ALONG THE SAND
OR LOUDLY DASH UPON THE STRAND:

YON GAILY RIGGED TRIM PLEASURE BOAT
UPON THE GLITTERING WAVES AFLOAT,
THEN (TURNING TO THE WEST) IS SEEN
DEAR CARTMEL'S PEACEFUL VALLEY GREEN;
MID WANING WOODS AND VERDANT LANDS;
THE FINE OLD CHURCH OF CARTMEL STANDS;

WITHIN WHOSE WALLS IN DAYS OF YORE
HIS PRIESTLY RULE THE PRIOR BORE;
THEN MAY THE LENGTHENED CHAIN AROUND
KEEP ONLY CATTLE FROM THE GROUND!
FOR NO GOOD MAN WOULD THINK IT PLEASURE
TO CLIMB THE FELL TO SPOIL YOUR TREASURE
YOUR OFFER MADE IN KINDLY SPIRIT
I HOPE YOU'LL FIND OUR CONDUCT MERIT:

CARTMEL 1846

A further notice warns against vandalism:

TAKE NOTICE

ALL PERSONS VISITING THIS "HOSPICE" BY PERMISSION
OF THE OWNER ARE REQUESTED TO RESPECT PRIVATE
PROPERTY, AND NOT BY ACTS OF WANTON MISCHIEF
AND DESTRUCTION SHOW THAT THEY POSSESS MORE
MUSCLE THAN BRAIN. I HAVE NO HOPE THAT THIS
REQUEST WILL BE ATTENDED TO, FOR AS SOLOMON SAYS
"THOUGH THOU SHOULDST BRAY A FOOL IN A MORTAR AMONGST
WHEAT WITH A PESTLE YET WILL NOT HIS FOOLISHNESS
DEPART FROM HIM"

G.REMINGTON

Outside the Hospice there is a curious inscription in Greek over the door lintel.

Before leaving the Hospice, a large cairn nearby is worthy of note. This marks the site of an ancient burial, and according to local tradition contains the bones of soldiers who fell in AD 96 in a battle between Dunmail, King of Cumbria, and Edmund, King of the invading Saxons. In more recent times, the men of Cartmel gathered here in November 1745 to repel Jacobite rebels who were believed to be in the district.

From Hampsfell Hospice round to Lindale our route is scenic in the extreme, with marvellous sweeping views, particularly of the Lake District. There is also much of interest to the botanist, the limestone clints containing exotic ferns, and the grasslands being richly carpeted with eyebright, tormentil and wild thyme. On the limestone grow gorse and juniper bushes. This kind of scrub-land is known locally as "savin". After following a gully down to a gate and continuing onwards through conifers we descend a while towards the road, but before reaching it double back sharply right, crossing fields to an old limekiln in an excellent state of preservation. Beyond a track leads round to Stonegarth, passing a postbox and an interesting covered well en route.

At Stonegarth a choice must be made. Beyond, our route descends steeply down to Lindale, but having visited Lindale you will have to retrace your steps to this point. A right turn takes us back to Eggerslack Woods and back down to Grange by a different route. The main attraction of Lindale, the Wilkinson Obelisk, stands beside the main road to Grange, and can be easily inspected by car. If the day is late, or you are tired, you would be wise to follow the latter option.

Lindale is a pleasant little village, straggling a steep fellside, with a small church, built by George Webster of Kendal who is buried in the churchyard in an elaborate grave. Mrs Gaskell lived here for a time while writing *The Sexton's Hero*, but Lindale is best known for its association with one of the founding fathers of the Industrial Revolution - John "Iron Mad" Wilkinson.

John Wilkinson was a powerful and extraordinary figure. Devious and rough-spoken, he was possessed of a foul temper and a political radicalism which did not endear him to his contemporaries. Wilkinson originated from the Penrith area, but at the age of twelve, in 1741, his family moved to nearby Backbarrow. At the age of 19 he purchased a furnace and forge at Wilson House, which lies near the present main road between Lindale and Levens Bridge. Here he invented the box iron, using an old mill in Lindale for processing his materials. Wilkinson built his own canal alongside the Winster, and built the world's first iron boat to carry peat and brick clay along it. People laughed at his "iron boat", confident it would sink, but Wilkinson proved them wrong! His fame and influence soon stretched far beyond sleepy Lindale, and most of his work took place in the Midlands. There can be no doubt that the genius of this wayward and eccentric man lay behind many of the innovations which made possible the Age of Steam.

When Wilkinson retired, he returned to Lindale and built himself a great Georgian mansion at nearby Castle Head with the proceeds of his industrial successes. This was an area of barren rock which Wilkinson domesticated into a garden paradise - an estate surrounded by a high, castellated wall. He originally employed local folk to work on this project, but as they would not work on Sundays he brought in large numbers of Irish navvies, whom he summoned with an ancient bell he had acquired from Cartmel Priory. On his death in 1801, Wilkinson willed that his body be buried in an iron coffin which he had long kept for the purpose. He was laid to rest in his own garden at Castle Head, his grave being topped by the massive iron Obelisk we now see in Lindale. Later tenants of Castle Head objected to having John Wilkinson at the bottom of their garden, and he was eventually exhumed and re-interred in the churchyard at Lindale. Not surprisingly the people of Lindale did not want Wilkinson's massive iron monument gracing their tiny churchyard, so iron master and iron obelisk were parted, the Obelisk remaining at Castlehead at a safe distance from hallowed ground.

But this was not the end of the Wilkinson saga, for the Obelisk was not fated to remain at Castle Head. In June 1983 it was moved from there and erected at its present position. In 1984 the parish council commissioned Dorothea Restoration Engineers Ltd of Buxton to restore the Obelisk, the cost being met by various grants and a nationwide appeal.

They did a good job. Today, Wilkinson's black iron monument gleams in its little triangular garden alongside the B5277 and Dixon Wood Close. On the side of the monument is a profile relief of Wilkinson himself, with the following inscription:

JOHN WILKINSON
IRON MASTER
WHO DIED XIV JULY, MDCCCVIIII
AGED LXXX YEARS
HIS DIFFERENT WORKS
IN VARIOUS PARTS OF THE
KINGDOM
ARE LASTING TESTIMONIES
OF HIS UNCEASING
LABOURS
HIS LIFE WAS SPENT IN
ACTION
FOR THE BENEFIT
OF MAN
AND, AS HE PRESUMED
HUMBLY TO HOPE
TO THE
GLORY OF GOD
LABORE ET HONORE.

Yet a part of the inscription is missing. If you look very carefully above the name of "John Wilkinson", you should just be able to make out the shapes of two words which have been carefully effaced from the Obelisk - "HERE LIES" - John Wilkinson and his obelisk are still parted.

So we come to the end of our journey. If you have not driven to Lindale, it is now time to retrace your steps back up to Stone Garth. As you ascend the hillside from Lindale, look out for the Eller How Tower, a sham ruin that stands atop Ravensbarrow Crag opposite. Back on Hampsfell, we follow a path along the top of Eggerslack Woods, before descending this delightful woodland once more by a different path, which, nevertheless, leads us eventually back to Grange. As with most of the walks on this side of Morecambe Bay, you are left with the feeling that there is much more to see than you actually saw, and the urge will be to return once again and explore further. Yet no matter how many times you return here, "oversands" Lancashire is an area that will always invite further exploration.

The Walk

Start on Windermere Road, Grange. Proceed along the road a short distance then turn left just past Blawith Lodge (1890), following a signed footpath up the wood. Ascend steps, cross a track, then continue onwards to a second set of steps and track (Point A), before joining the well signed path up through Eggerslack Woods which passes a seat and some curious concrete pits before finally reaching a seat and stile at the top of the wood.

Continue onto the open fell, ascending by limestone clints to a cairn by a tree. Soon a stile appears in the wall (on the left). Pass through, and follow the wall to its corner. Continue onwards over open ground, until Hampsfell Hospice appears over the rise.

At the Hospice bear right, following an indistinct path along the fell until a gully is encountered. Bear left along the gully, following a path which soon descends to a wall stile and small gate leading into conifers. Continue onwards, passing between two large boulders, before descending left to a wallside. At the end of the wall pass through the gate into the pasture and bear right, until a small stile appears in the wall (on the right). Pass through this to a further stile, beyond which a lime kiln appears on the right. Beyond the kiln, a track is joined which leads unerringly to farm buildings. Pass through the farm bearing left then right onto a metalled lane which leads to Stonegarth.

Pass to the left of Stonegarth to a gate and a stile. Descend the pasture to another stile, beyond which a kissing gate gives access to woods. Pass the remains of a second kissing gate, cross a private road to a third, then descend steeply down towards Lindale, where a squeezer stile gives access to Lingarth by a substation. Descend through housing, bear left, and cross to a lane. Then, passing the church on the left, descend to the primary school with its belltower, just beyond Hoosa Crag. Turn right, down the side of the primary school, and descend to Millgarth. Turn right into playing fields and pass public toilets to the main road. Cross to view the Lindale Obelisk, which stands opposite at the junction with Dixon Wood Close.

Retrace your steps to Stonegarth. Bear left behind Stonegarth, following a signed footpath to Hampsfell. Pass through a gate then through a stile in the wall on the left, which enters woodland. Pass through a second stile (with wall now on the left again). Where the wall veers to the right, pass through a gate into Eggerslack Woods.

Ignoring paths to the left and right, the route descends without complication to the road. Do not turn left into the road. Instead bear right up a track which ascends slightly before meeting the outward route at point A. Turn left and descend the wood back to Windermere Road.

15: HUMPHREY HEAD AND THE KIRKHEAD TOWER

Humphrey Head is the highest (and just about only) cliff of any size on the Lancashire coast. The Kirkhead Tower stands above it, offering excellent views over Morecambe Bay. Together they add up to a scenic and most interesting walk.

Getting there:	A590 then the B5277 through Grange-over-Sands to Allithwaite
Distance:	7 miles approx.
Map refs:	Allithwaite SD 386 762, Kirkhead Tower SD 393 756 Landranger 97
Rating:	Walk ** Follies and General Interest *

Our walk starts at the picturesque little village of Allithwaite by the Pheasant Inn (patrons car park behind). This clustered little community, which stands on the southern slopes of Hampsfell midway between Grange and Cartmel, appears in old records as Hailinethwait, and the name is believed to be derived from the old English *Halig Wella* - "the clearing by the Holy Well". This name makes sense, as we are shortly to encounter the said "Holy Well" on our way to Humphrey Head. It is also worth considering the possibility that the name is in fact Old Norse and means simply "Halle's son's clearing".

Allithwaite was traditionally a community of fishermen, while at Blenket Farm the only iron ore mine in the area was worked, the ore being taken to Backbarrow to be melted down. Today Allithwaite seems to be in danger of becoming a suburb of Grange. We can only hope that the village manages to retain its identity somehow.

From Allithwaite we pass over a series of flat fields to a lane before encountering our first place of interest by a bend in the road. A few hundred yards up a farm track, incongruously sited in the midst of a farmyard, stand the tall, gaunt ruins of Wraysholme Tower.

Wraysholme Tower is a mediaeval pele tower, which was built,

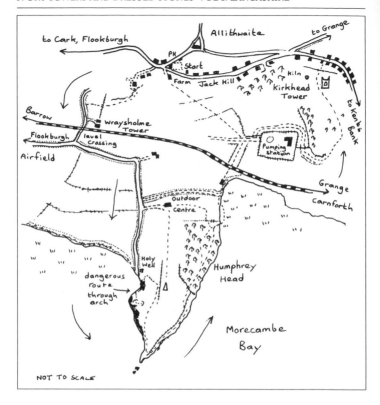

along with its near neighbours Arnside and Hazelslack Towers, to withstand the incursions into this area of the ravaging Scots who repeatedly invaded Northern England after Bannockburn, burning and plundering the Furness area in 1322. Wraysholme Tower is not open or accessible to the public, being part of the farm, so it must therefore be inspected from a distance.

The tower reputedly dates from around 1485 (although some sources place it as far back as the thirteenth century) and it originally had a hall attached to it on its north side. It is 39 feet high, and the projecting turret at the south-west angle contains the tower's Garde Robe (lavatory). The tower is built of rough rubble limestone and

Humphrey Head

the walls are 4 feet thick, reputedly cemented together with lime and bullock's blood. It was obviously designed to withstand a great deal. Comfort was sacrificed to the needs of defence, but as the building (like its sister towers) was never intended to be much more than a defensive lookout tower and an occasional hunting lodge for its owner, its comfort would not have been a major consideration anyway.

The tower was built by the Harringtons of Gleaston, who in the Middle Ages were wardens of the coast. They were a powerful and influential family with far-flung estates, Sir William Harrington of Hornby Castle being Henry V's standard bearer at Agincourt. Besides Wraysholme they also held Farleton, Arnside and Hazelslack Towers. During the Wars of the Roses, however, they fared rather badly, mainly as a result of supporting Richard III, who was a popular figure in the North. After Bosworth Field and their equally ill-starred support for the Yorkist "pretender" Lambert Simnel (who landed on nearby Piel Island in June 1487), the estates of Sir James Harrington and his brother were seized and handed over to the Stanleys, who, as any reader of Shakespeare knows, had, during the Battle of Bosworth switched sides at the last minute and given Henry Tudor the victory. The Stanleys (later the Earls of Derby) eventually sold off Raisholme to the Dicconson family, who held it for a time, but eventually the tower passed to humbler owners and was gradually allowed to fall into ruin. Today it functions as a farm building. Its cressets have given way to TV aerials, and its lonely sentinels to clucking chickens: an ignominious fate indeed.

Continuing on our route we cross the railway. At a junction we bear left, then follow the lane round to the rocky bulwark of Humphrey Head, which juts out onto the sands of Morecambe Bay. Humphrey Head is the only sea cliff of any note between North Wales and St Bees. 160 feet high, its precipices - thanks to the sands and low lying coastline all around - look higher than they actually are. From the triangulation point on the summit of the headland, there is a fine prospect taking in the Pennines, the Bowlands and Lancaster; The Ashton Memorial and Blackpool Tower are also both in view. At low tide it is possible to walk right around the headland on the beach, but it is worth remembering that when the tide does come in it comes in amazingly fast, and flows right up to the base of the cliff. If in doubt, follow the top route.

Humphrey Head offers much of interest. According to legend it was the scene of a famous "chase" (immortalised in poem and ballad) in which the last wolf was slain by one of the Harringtons of Wraysholme Tower. By all accounts, Sir Edgar Harrington offered the hand of Adela, his niece, to anyone who would rid the district of the last wolf in Cumbria. A mysterious stranger duly dispatched the creature, and upon revealing his true identity turned out to be Sir Edgar's long lost son and Adela's banished sweetheart.

At the end of the lane, near the base of the cliff stand the now pathetic remains of St Agnes Well, the stone hut which formerly covered it being long ago reduced to ruin. The Holy Well of St Agnes has an interesting history. In the eighteenth and nineteenth centuries it was popular as a spa, and the salty waters were said to cure ague, gout, jaundice and worms. Lead miners from Alston Moor in

Northumberland made an annual pilgrimage to the well, believing that it countered the effects of lead poisoning, and its waters were also poured into milk kits and carried by rail to Morecambe to be sold to holidaymakers.

From the end of the lane, hard by the beach, a steep path ascends through the woods at the base of the cliff, becoming a rock scramble as it winds right to the cliff top. Further along the base of the cliff an even more precipitous path leads up, passing through a natural "window" in the rock. Would-be climbers would be wise to take heed of the following warning which is carved on a rock at the base of the cliff:

> Beware how you these rocks ascend
> Here WILLIAM PEDDER met his end
>
> August 22nd 1857 Aged 10 years
>
> *By Permission*

After seeking out and exploring the Fairy Chapel Cave, our route passes through the coppice wood on the eastern side of the headland, before skirting sea marshes to reach cottages and a low tunnel beneath the railway line. Here the rails are in view immediately above you as you pass underneath - it must be a thrilling experience to be there when a train is passing directly overhead!

Beyond the railway, a choice must be made. The public footpath leads directly back to Allithwaite across some marshy fields, but a right turn gives access to a track which leads directly around the perimeter of the treatment plant and onto the flanks of Kirkhead. Although not shown as a right of way, this route is obviously used by horse riders, and therefore seems a reasonably safe bet for walkers. (If you are squeamish, you can return to Allithwaite and visit Kirkhead from the other side, having gone round by road.)

Kirkhead is an interesting eminence. Strictly speaking it is an outlier of Hampsfell, although it is cut off from that hillside by the road and houses which are strung out to the north of it. Nestling under Kirkhead on the Kents Bank side is Abbots Hall, which was where the Abbot of Furness used to stop over when making the arduous journey across the sands from Furness Abbey to his extensive holdings in Yorkshire. Today a Methodist guest house stands on the site.

In the southern face of Kirkhead is Kirkhead Cave (which I was unable to find on my visit). It is, by all accounts, quite well hidden in the wood scrubland and, I am informed, stands about 80 feet above the high water mark in a low limestone scar. Its entrance is only 2 feet high, but inside it rises to 14 feet and gives access to a series of caverns in the limestone. Large quantities of prehistoric bones, both human and animal, have been found in these caves along with potsherds, jewellery, a bronze spearhead and a coin dating from the time of the Emperor Domitian (AD 84). Animal bones found included those of red deer, wildcat, fox and boar. One item of interest was the metatarsal bone of a pig which had been carved into a whistle.

On the summit of Kirkhead lies the chief object of our journey, the Kirkhead Tower which has been in view for much of our walk. I can offer little in the way of hard information about it. It was built originally as a summer house, and its Gothic character would suggest that it dates from the nineteenth century. The views from it are, as one might expect, quite spectacular, and it is occasionally used as a venue for outdoor Sunday morning worship, its steps and arched window forming a perfect open air pulpit. According to legend, the tower was built on the site of an ancient church which, in the days before the building of Cartmel Priory, served as an oratory for the devotions of travellers. This modern usage, therefore, is quite apt. It is from this vanished chapel that the hilltop - "Kirkhead" - supposedly derives its name.

From the tower, we make our way to the Kents Bank road, passing a fine lime kiln on the slope below us. A left turn from the road leads us down through an area of housing to the start of our walk at the Pheasant Inn, where, with a pint of best bitter, you can make a pleasant end to an intricate and interesting ramble.

The Walk

Start at the Pheasant Inn, Allithwaite. At the road junction pass a post box on your left, and within a few yards descend to the left down a signed lane, passing conifers on the left. At the second group of cottages bear right then left onto a diverted footpath, which leads around the cottages to a kissing gate and footbridge. Cross the stream and turn right, following the bank of the stream to an iron swing gate, beyond which another stile leads into the lane. Turn left.

Proceed along the lane passing Wraysholme Tower on the left. Cross over the railway and at the road junction bear left. The road runs straight for some distance, crossing a beck before bearing right near a farm road and a lime kiln. From here follow Holy Well Lane down to the beach.

From the beach a steep scramble leads up the cliff to the triangulation pillar on the top of Humphrey Head. Further along the beach, an even steeper scramble leads up through a rock window to the top of the cliff - but this must be negotiated with extreme care, and is not recommended. From the triangulation pillar continue onwards, follow a fence on the right to the end of the point. Bear left around the point to where a ladder stile gives access to woodland. Proceed through the wood, with the shoreline on the right, ignoring a path leading off left. At the end of the wood, near a gate signed Private bear right down to the shoreline, then turn left along the wallside, heading towards the railway with salt marshes on your right. Soon the walled lane across the headland appears on the left. Continue onwards, following the wall, until, just beyond a cottage, a wall stile appears on the left. Pass over it, turn right, and pass under the railway. Continue onwards until a track is joined, which leads off right to a water treatment works. Here a choice must be made.

There is no certain right of way onto Kirkhead, so (if in doubt) continue onwards, where a public footpath leads directly back to the Pheasant Inn via a farmyard.

16: THE ULVERSTON FOLLIES

On this long walk we visit a sham lighthouse, a ship canal, a Buddhist institute, a mysterious triangular mausoleum and a house associated with the founder of Quakerism. Also featured are fine views to the Lake District, a seaside stroll and last, but by no means least,"Stan and Ollie".

Getting there:	From M6 Junction 36, follow the A591 a short distance then turn onto the A590 Barrow-in-Furness trunk road. Drive to Ulverston via Newby Bridge. Park in the town centre.
Distance:	14 miles approx.
Map refs:	SD 285 785, Hoad Monument 295 791 Landranger 97
Rating:	Walk *** Follies and General Interest ***

Conishead Priory is open from 1-5 pm Sat/Sun/Bank Holidays, Easter to the end of September. House tours are available and there is a souvenir shop and coffee bar.

Ulverston is perhaps the most distant outpost of former Lancashire to be visited in our search for follies. Situated on low ground between the sands of the Leven Estuary and the rocky outliers of the Lakeland Fells, this cozy little town straddles the busy Barrow-in-Furness trunk road. Today, like the rest of "oversands" Lancashire, Ulverston belongs to Cumbria, but it traditionally owed its identity to its position at the terminus of the old coach route across the sands from Lancaster, the crossing of the Leven estuary from Flookburgh being the last leg of what was once a long and hazardous journey.

Certainly Ulverston has ancient roots. Its name appears in the *Domesday Book*, and the original settlement is believed to be Saxon. In the twelfth century it was owned by Stephen of Blois (Henry I's nephew), but eventually it became the property of Furness Abbey, whose monks retained it up to the Dissolution. Most of present day Ulverston, is of eighteenth-century origin. It enjoyed such an immense prosperity that the town once boasted the title of the

Conishead Priory
The Temple, Ince Blundell

Darwen Tower

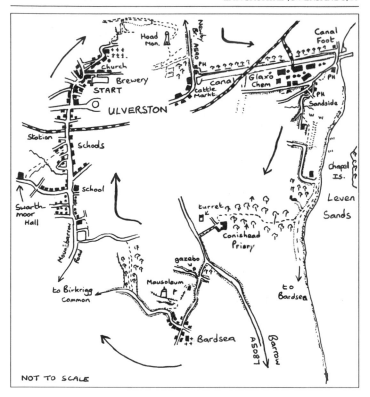

NOT TO SCALE

"London" of Furness. Much of this prosperity was due to the arrival of the Ulverston Canal in 1759, which encouraged the town's development as a port, and the construction of the turnpike in 1763. By the mid nineteenth century the canal had been eclipsed by the Furness Railway, yet the town's prosperity remained undiminished as it continued to sell its slate, cotton, leather and ore.

Today Ulverston's biggest employer is the Glaxo chemical plant, which lies alongside the canal to the east of the town. There is also a thriving tourist industry. Ulverston's street markets, held on Thursdays and Saturdays, attract the crowds, and there is also a livestock auction on the Thursday, which is known locally as "L'ile

The Hoad Hill Monument

Pig Day". Tourists also flock to Ulverston's Laurel and Hardy Museum, for Stan Laurel was born here in Argyle Street in 1890.

This particular walk is quite a long one, so prepare well. Our route starts out along Church Walk, passing an interesting little gazebo on the left, at a junction of lanes. Soon we approach the entrance gates to St Mary's Church, which is older than it looks. The first church here was built in 1111, and the building is locally called the "church of the four ones" in consequence. Little now remains from this period apart from the south door.

Behind the church, we discover a footpath which leads up onto Hoad Hill, eventually joining a track which leads unerringly round to the Hoad Hill Monument, a structure which offers no surprises, dominating Ulverston to such an extent that there is no way you can enter the town without seeing it.

The Hoad Hill Monument (sometimes known as the Hoade) looks like a lighthouse but that was not, and never has been, its purpose. It was erected to commemorate the Under-Secretary to the Admiralty, Sir John Barrow, the famous geographer and writer who died in 1848 at the age of 84. He was born in 1764 in a little cottage at Dragley Beck, and was educated at the local grammar school. Barrow was good at maths; at the age of 13 he was selected to assist in a survey of the Conishead Priory Estates, and at 14 he took up an appointment at a Liverpool Iron Works, working as wages clerk. From such humble beginnings he rose to greatness, being Secretary of the Admiralty from 1804 to 1845.

After his death, two committees were formed to erect a monument to his memory. One consisted of various naval dignitaries and the other was a local committee. The proposed monument, designed by A.Trimen, was intended to be a land-locked replica of the Eddystone Lighthouse. Soon £1000 had been raised for the project, among the list of subscribers being HM Queen Dowager, I.K.Brunel and Sir Robert Peel. It is interesting to note that Trinity House donated £100 to the scheme, with the strict proviso that the monument be made available for use as a lighthouse if so required.

The site chosen for the monument, on top of Hoad Hill, was originally the site of Ulverston's traditional 5th November bonfire. Ulverston, it seems celebrated the occasion not with a Guy Fawkes, but with the burning in effigy of unpopular local officials, shopkeepers and so on, the 'victims' first being paraded through the streets accompanied by a jeering mob.

The foundation stones of the monument were laid on 15th May 1850. Early in the morning the church bells were rung, and the Ulverston town band set up in the market place. By 8 am the band was in full swing and hundreds of people had already gathered for the day's festivities. At 1 pm a procession, by now several thousand strong, set off up Hoad Hill. After passing through a succession of flower-bedecked arches, the crowd finally reached the summit of the hill, and a short service was held. In a cavity beneath the foundation stone was buried a bottle containing all the coin denominations of the day and a copy of the *Ulverston Advertiser*. Then the stone was finally laid amidst loud cheers. This was followed by prayers, more cheers and numerous speeches, before the crowds, now numbering about 8,000, wound their way back down to partake of the numerous specially-prepared meals waiting for them in Ulverston! It was, it seems, rather a hectic day for the little town.

The monument was completed by the end of 1850. The final cost was £1,250. Once more bells rang, flags waved and the workmen were feasted in the tower. All that remained was to erect the

131

lightning conductor, but this was put off to be done at a later date, and the scaffolding was taken down.

Such a blatant disregard of Murphy's Law was asking for trouble, and sure enough, on 30th January 1851 just twenty-seven days after completion, a freak storm blew up and lightning seriously damaged the monument. Nine massive blocks cut loose, four of them falling outside and damaging the buttresses, the rest falling into the tower smashing six iron girders, two landings, and numerous steps. The top cupola, it transpired, had moved, and consequently the whole upper part of the tower had to be rebuilt, at a cost of £136. During this restoration James Riley, a waller, fell from a broken step into the central well and was seriously injured.

So the monument was completed once more (this time with its lightning conductor), but it was not long left unmolested, for by July of that same year there were reports of vandalism. To rectify this problem a door was fitted to the 100 foot tower and a charge made to ascend the 122 steps and to enjoy the view with the high powered telescope especially installed for the purpose. There were originally three keys to the monument, one held by the Barrow family, one by the tenant of the land and the other by the town trustees. Nowadays the tower is open to the public when the flag is raised.

But you don't need the tower to enjoy the prospect, which looks southwards across Morecambe Bay to Heysham, and northwards to the Lakeland mountains. Ingleborough can be seen, and there are sweeping views across the Leven and Crake estuaries. Nearer at hand is Ulverston, and a fine view down the coast to Chapel Island and to Conishead Priory surrounded by its trees. From Hoad Hill you can plan out the rest of the walk before you undertake it. A steep, rocky descent leads down to the road and the canal, which we follow for its full length down to the bay at Canal Foot. In summer the 1^{1}/4 mile stroll along the bank is a long, leafy corridor, seemingly stretching to infinity.

The Ulverston Canal was essentially a ship canal - Ulverston's link with the sea. Built in 1795 by John Rennie, it was in its heyday the shortest, straightest and deepest canal in England. Through the sea lock at Canal Foot was shipped Ulverston's iron ore and manufactured goods, creating a golden age of prosperity which made Ulverston the premier port in Furness. The Railway Age and the development of the great docks at Barrow forced the Ulverston Canal into a tranquil retirement. Today the canal is left alone with its memories.

From Canal Foot, the "oversands" footpath leads across Cartmel Sands to Flookburgh. This is not a walk to be undertaken without a guide. The tide is usually out, but when it does come in, it does so with amazing speed! Swift, treacherous and grey, the waters of Morecambe Bay are not to be trifled with! Lives have been lost hereabouts, and if you happen to be here around high tide, it is not difficult to see why.

Leaving Canal Foot with its pub (the Bay Horse), picnic sites and jetty, our route follows the lane round to Sandside; and then beyond Saltcotes Farm we take to a route which leads back towards the sands, eventually joining a footpath which runs along the coast towards Bardsea. The small island offshore is Chapel Island, which once served as a refuge for travellers crossing the sands. Its mediaeval chapel was converted into a sham ruined eyecatcher by Colonel Bradyll of Conishead Priory (of whom more shortly). A vicious storm turned it into a real ruin in 1984.

From the beach we follow a well defined and pleasant woodland path into the grounds of Conishead Priory. The whole estate is private, but both house and grounds are open to the public, who are encouraged to roam at will. Various exotic trees are to be found in the grounds, and the American Garden includes an atlas cedar and a giant redwood. There is a nature trail and seventy acres of woods and gardens.

Conishead Priory is an architectural work of art or a "Gothick" monstrosity - it depends on your point of view. Certainly it is stunning, worthy of being dubbed a folly in its own right. It was built for Colonel T.R.Gale Bradyll of the Coldstream Guards by Philip Wyatt at a cost of £140,000, and took from 1821 to 1836 to build. The project was so expensive that Bradyll had to sell the estate to cover the bill. The end result of all this labour was one of the most outstanding examples of the Gothic revival in Britain. Its turrets are 100 feet high and it contains a gloomy cloister corridor 170 feet long. Colonel Braddyl did not stop here, however. He filled his house with art treasures - Rembrandts and Titians hung from every wall.

Of course this was not the first building on the site. The original priory was a foundation of Black (Augustinian) Canons who had succeeded to a small community originally founded as a leper hospital by Gamel De Pennington around 1160. Besides ministering to the poor and the needy, the canons also maintained a guide to lead travellers over the sands, and it was they who built the chapel on Chapel Island. Conishead Priory must have been a very small foundation, for at the Dissolution its lead, bells and timber were all sold for less than £400. Thereafter it became a private residence, the last of a series of houses being demolished in 1821 to make way for the Colonel Bradyll's fantastic creation.

The present priory has had rather a chequered career. Colonel Bradyll went bankrupt twelve years after its completion, and at one stage it was used as a hydropathic hotel. In 1929 it was sold to the Coal Board and the Durham Miner's Welfare Committee for £35,000. They converted the house into a convalescent home at a further cost of £22,000. In 1972 the miners left, and the priory was bought by a Preston entrepreneur who sought to convert the house and grounds into a motel and a site for 300 caravans. Not surprisingly, planning permission was refused, and the house was left empty for five years, during which time it became dilapidated, much of the fabric being attacked by dry rot. Demolition suddenly became an option.

Yet mercifully Conishead Priory has since acquired a new lease of life - as a Tibetan Buddhist community. In 1976 it was purchased by the Manjushri Institute, who have done much towards restoring the house to its former glory. Today, the first thing that greets you as you enter its portals is an enormous statue of Buddha, colourful and serene. The priory is now a college and a community, given over to a very alternative lifestyle. Here there is peace, meditation, tranquillity - and self-reliance. History has come full circle and one feels that the Black Canons would almost certainly have approved. Conishead Priory is a "priory" once more.

While Colonel Bradyll was having his house built, he amused himself by building lesser follies. We have already mentioned the eyecatcher on Chapel Island, and nearby on Hermitage Hill he built a tower, octagonal and machicolated, with a turret and cross-shaped arrow slits. This tower is now owned by Mr Roger Fisher, a local racehorse trainer, who is engaged in restoring it.

And so we proceed on towards Bardsea and the final folly on our

Mausoleum , Bardsea

journey, a triangular Mausoleum standing on a high limestone pavement at the top end of Bardsea Golf Club. Permission to inspect may be obtained at the clubhouse, although one suspects that they do not approve of non-golfers walking alongside the fairway.

The Mausoleum is certainly worth the detour. It is a folly in the classic eighteenth-century style - triangular with corner buttresses, corbels, corner pyramids and a central cupola. It contains three niches, one of which contains a sepulchral urn. According to the National Trust book of follies, it was the last of Colonel Bradyll's "conceits", his last resting place, a building descended from the wild Irish follies of the eighteenth century, in the manner of Thomas Wright's Tollymore follies. Here is a mystery. On one side of this triangular building is an urn with a weathered, almost unreadable inscription, yet enough of it is legible to betray a definite eighteenth-century date. But Bradyll was building in the mid nineteenth century. Could this mausoleum have been the creation of the preceding generation of Bradylls? Unfortunately I have not been able to acquire any detailed information about this intriguing and mysterious structure, so who actually built it, must, for the time being at least, remain a mystery.

After a pleasant footpath through woods, our route joins the lane back to Ulverston, and on reaching the outer suburbs of the town we are faced with a tiring tarmac slog back to the start of the walk. If time (and energy!) permit you can make an interesting diversion to Swarthmoor Hall, one of the earliest shrines of Quakerism. The house was the abode of Judge Fell, a friend of George Fox, and Fox stayed at Swarthmoor in the 1650s. Today the house is owned by the Society of Friends and is open for public inspection.

So we come to the end of what has been a long, but highly interesting perambulation. Sea and sands, crags and mountain vistas, not to mention an interesting little town, have all featured in our journey. A long walk, but well worth the effort.

The Walk

Start at Fountain Street car park Ulverston. Turn left onto Fountain Street and proceed to the road junction by the King's Arms. Turn sharp right onto Church Walk, passing the bowling club and an interesting little gazebo by the junction with Ainsworth Street. Continue to St Mary's Church. Pass to the left of the church up Green Bank, then follow the road, bearing to the right, behind the church.

At a sign (Hoad Hill) turn left up a short lane to a kissing gate and cross diagonally to a second kissing gate, following an enclosed path which soon opens out, crossing a track by seats. Continue uphill to a walled-in section of path with two more kissing gates, bearing right to join a track which leads around the hillside by seats and rock outcrops to the Hoad Hill Monument.

From the monument descend steeply to a mock stone circle by seats. Bear right (ignoring a path to the left) to a large kissing gate which gives access to Church Walk. Turn left. and descend to the A590. At the main road, turn right towards Ulverston, passing a garage. Cross the main road, and follow a lane which leads down the side of the Canal Tavern, passing a scrapyard on the left. This lane leads arrow straight for about a mile to Canal Foot.

At Canal Foot, turn right over the canal towards the Bay Horse then right again, following the road towards Sandside, passing chemical works on the right. At Sandside turn right to the Seaview public house, beyond which a small lane leads past Saltcotes Farm.

Beyond the stream bear left through a kissing gate, following a path which eventually joins a lane by an old chimney. Continue onwards bearing left past a cottage to regain the shoreline. Turn right along the shore for a short distance, then right again, entering a woodland trail which leads to Conishead Priory.

From the Priory, bear left, following a drive to the A5087, noting a Castellated Folly (private) on the right. At the main road bear left then right, following the lane towards Bardsea, noting a small gazebo in the field on the right. At the edge of Bardsea turn right, along a lane signed Urswick. About half a mile along bear right through a kissing gate, following a well defined path through woodland. The Mausoleum is visible on the hilltop (right). Beyond a kissing gate leave the woods and follow a well defined path to a tarmac lane. Bear left along the lane a short distance, then right, through Middle Mount Barrow, passing a footpath signed To Priory Road on the right. Take the next path on the right which leads to the Ulverston road at Croftlands. Follow the road towards Ulverston, diverting off left down Swarthmoor Hall Lane to Swarthmoor Hall if desired. From Swarthmoor a path leads across the Levy Back back towards Ulverston. Pass Ulverston Station on the left then, after crossing the A590, continue onwards through Ulverston to the Kings Arms. Bear right for Fountain Street and your car.

Gazebo between Conishead and Bardsea

APPENDIX

Accrington - Eyecatcher, New High Riley. Landranger 103 location uncertain.

Georgian eyecatcher tower with quatrefoil windows.

Belmont - Holymosside Tower. Landranger 109, location uncertain.

Eighteenth-century, 62 feet high and reputedly haunted. Perhaps the tower itself is a ghost because I can't find it!

Bury - Map ref: SD 802 108 Landranger 109.

Bury's finest jewel is its Kay Monument at the south end of Market Street. A pavilion with a stone dome surmounted by a bronze frame, this was erected to the memory of John Kay, inventor of the "Flying Shuttle" which was so instrumental in the Industrial Revolution. Kay was born in Bury in 1704. A bronze portrait of Kay in relief surmounts a panel containing an inscription. On either side of the monument are depictions of a power loom and a hand loom. Adjacent to the monument is a fine drinking fountain, presented to the town by John Barlow JP of Wellfield in 1907.

Bury also has a fine Clock Tower built in memory of Walter Whitehead, a Manchester surgeon. It is stone-built and square, and was designed by Maxwell and Tuke in 1914. It has four keep-like turrets.

Capernwray - The Gamekeeper's Tower. Map ref: SD 542 714 Landranger 97.

The nineteenth-century Gothic tower near Capernwray Hall is in a ruinous condition and needs to be saved before it is too late. Access to it involves locating a decayed and rarely-used footpath, which leads up the hillside from the nearby Hobsons Caravan Park. The walk is a pleasant stroll with nearby woodlands and a possible chance of sighting red deer. It is not, however, a substantial enough walk to merit a full chapter in this book. You could perhaps take it in en route to the Pepperpot which lies not too far distant at Silverdale.

Little is known about the Capernwray Tower. It belonged to the estate of nearby Capernwray Hall, being built by Mr George Marton (the builder of the present Capernwray Hall) as a lookout tower and a residence for his head gamekeeper. The tower is a listed building, and prior to its present ruinous condition was used by the Boy Scouts. In 1979 it was reported at a parish council meeting that the tower had been vandalised, and its state has progressively worsened since. According to the local farmer the tower is still frequented by vandals, which seems surprising, considering the remote location of the place. Successive Martons lived at Capernwray Hall until death duties forced them to sell the house in 1946 for the princely sum of £7,350. Today the hall is a young people's Christian holiday conference centre.

To reach the tower, start at the bend in the road just above the entrance gates to Capernwray Hall. A few yards down the road by a ruined barn a stile on the left gives access to a footpath which leads between walls to a second stile. Enter the field and turn left across pasture to a gate in the fence (no stile, and gate is fastened). Proceed towards farm buildings but instead of heading for the gate, bear slightly left uphill where a "stride over" stile leads through an overgrown area of newly planted "whips", to a finely wrought stile in the stone wall opposite, which joins a lane opposite the entrance to a caravan park. Turn right, down the lane a few yards, then left, passing in front of the farmhouse (paved terrace and ornamental lamps). Beyond, a couple of steps lead into dense undergrowth where an overgrown path bears slightly right around the edge of the garden to a stile by a stream. Pass over the footbridge then turn left, following the fence up the pasture to a stile in the top left-hand corner. Pass through the stile and proceed a short distance up the field to the Hunting tower. After examining the folly retrace your steps to the start of the walk.

Clitheroe - Parliament Turret. Map ref: SD 742 417
Landranger 103.

Castle Gardens, Clitheroe. Situated in the rose garden just beneath the Castle Museum, this small folly is actually a refugee turret from the Houses of Parliament in London. It originally formed part of that building and was presented to Clitheroe by Captain Sir William Brass, MP.

Colne - The Wallace Hartley Memorial. Landranger 103, exact location uncertain.

This bust on a plinth was erected to the memory of the bandmaster of the Titanic who went down with that ill-fated ship on 15th April 1912. Apparently Hartley led his band in a rendition of the hymn "Nearer my God to Thee" as the liner slid beneath the waves!

Colne -　　　　Walton Spire. Map ref: SD 895 374 Landranger 103. This obscure folly is to be found in a field by a junction of lanes to the south-east of the ancient fort of Castercliff, which straddles the hillside between Nelson and Colne. Looking like a refugee turret from a church cross-bred with a signpost, this has to be one of the oddest follies in Lancashire. Only its scale lets it down. Had it been massive, with perhaps an internal staircase and viewing platform, it would perhaps have been the wonder of the area, but alas, its smallness renders it quite unspectacular. A modern plaque (now unhappily smashed) informs us that the spire was constructed by one Richard Wroe Walton in 1835, on the site of an ancient monolith.

(His reason for doing so is not made clear.) In January 1984 the monument was toppled by a gale, which resulted in a petition being sent by local residents to the Mayor of Pendle pleading for its restoration, which was eventually achieved in 1985. The inscription on the spire is a curious one (it has to be read around the monument):

AD 1835
STR:FECt
R.T. WROE
WALTON

Walton Spire, Colne

> HA.COL
> AG:SHEL
> REG:CIR
> INDICA
> AD1835

Make of it what you will.

Delph - Denshaw Monument. Map ref: SD 968 082 Landranger 109.

Obelisk on hillside near Grains Bar (picnic and parking areas).

Far Sawrey - The Station. By Lake Windermere. Map ref: SD 388 955 Landranger 97.

This sad castellated ruin (now in Cumbria) was once a popular Victorian resort, serving as a viewpoint over the lake. It was built early in the last century by the Rev William Braithwaite to amuse his friends. The building was once white, octagonal with a castellated roof, and two storeys high. The ground floor was a dining room with an adjacent wine cellar, while upstairs a drawing room was lit by a six-sided bay window. This contained various panes of coloured

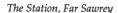

The Station, Far Sawrey

glass, through which, it is related, visitors were able to enjoy the view through the different "seasons". There was also a dark blue pane to simulate "moonlight" and a violet one to imitate a thunderstorm. In the 1830s and 1840s the building was a popular venue for dances, and was even visited by Queen Adelaide in 1840. No doubt there was many a romantic encounter here in those halcyon days when the pathways were lit up with Chinese lanterns and a salon orchestra was brought in from Kendal. The Station is, alas, somewhat bleaker today.

Further up the hill heading towards Claife Heights, there is supposed to be a Summerhouse known as Belle View, also built by the Rev William Braithwaite in 1799, but this seems to have been swallowed up by a private coniferous forest.

Finsthwaite   Spire. Map ref: SD 356 865 Landranger 97.
In Spire Wood, not far from Finsthwaite (see Finsthwaite Tower). A flattened obelisk. Origin unknown.

Fleetwood -   The Lighthouses. Map ref: SD 338 487
                    Landranger 102.
Although not strictly speaking follies, Fleetwood's two land based lighthouses are most certainly unusual, being quite different from what you would normally expect. Both are the work of Decimus Burton, the top London architect who was responsible for designing much of Fleetwood, which from the outset was very much a "planned" town. The lighthouses were originally gas-lit before being converted to electricity, and were intended to help boats navigate the Wyre Channel. The Lower Lighthouse is situated on the seafront, a classical structure incorporating a balustrade, columns and a shelter with seats. It is constructed of Stourton Hill white stone. The Upper Lighthouse just beyond it is known as the Pharos Lighthouse, because it was designed to be a replica of the Pharos of Alexandria, that famous lighthouse that was held to be one of the Seven Wonders of the Ancient World. Fleetwood's version is, I suspect, somewhat less impressive, being a red sandstone column standing some 90 feet above the high water level.

Gisburn -   Map ref: SD 827 498 Landranger 103.
Sham castle dog kennels, also temple by River Ribble on private land.

Grange-over-Sands - Holme Island. Map ref: SD 423 782
Landranger 97.

This rocky "island" sticking out into the sands, which is in fact connected to the "mainland" by a raised roadway, contains gardens, fountains, urns and a circular Temple of Vesta, supported by sixteen Corinthian pillars and adorned with five panel paintings. All of this could once be explored by tourists from Grange on payment of a one shilling. Today the whole estate is STRICTLY PRIVATE.

Grange-over-Sands - Longlands Tower. Map ref: SD 39 79
Landranger 97, exact location uncertain.

Little is known about this two-storeyed castellated Gothic tower, probably built for the Longlands Estate. Ruinous. Similar in appearance to the nearby Kirkhead Tower (see walk 15 p126).

Great Harwood - Mercer Memorial. Map ref:SD 734 327
Landranger 103.

The Mercer Memorial is a free-standing clock tower in the centre of Great Harwood, which was erected to the memory of John Mercer, Great Harwood's most famous son. Mercer, an industrial chemist, was the inventor of the mercerization process which gave cotton a highly attractive, silk-like sheen. Mercer was elected a Fellow of the Royal Society in 1852, and the memorial was erected in 1903 to mark his contribution to the development of Great Harwood.

Ince Blundell - Hall. Map ref: SD 326 029 Landranger 108,
south-east of Formby.

Ince Blundell is a delight. Its parkland (petite by eighteenth-century standards!) is surrounded by a rusty red brick wall, which screens it from the hum and clamour of the adjacent busy main road. Inside the wall is another world - a place of woods, gardens and quiet peaceful seclusion. Ince Blundell Hall is now a convalescent home. It is not public (which accounts for its peace and quiet) but neither is it private, and with the exception of a small garden containing a pavilion, you can stroll around the grounds and lakeside undisturbed.

Ince Blundell Hall was built in 1777, when Henry Blundell decided to replace his old Tudor hall with an up-to-date mansion. Blundell was a dedicated art collector, much travelled on the Continent, and rather than fill his house with his treasures he

The Lion Gate, Ince Blundell

decided to design two buildings especially for the purpose. The larger of these, The Pantheon, is attached to the far side of the hall, and was built to house Blundell's collection of antiquities, paintings and drawings. It is circular and fronted with a severely Classical portico. To house his collection of sculptures, Blundell built a fine Garden Temple, also looking to all intents and purposes like a refugee from ancient Rome. It is constructed of red brick with a portico of four Tuscan columns, and antique reliefs. It was designed by William Everard of Liverpool and constructed about 1780. Originally a greenhouse stood behind it, and it is to this that the inscription refers:

"HIC VER ASSIDUUM ATQUE ALIENIS MENSIBUS AESTAS".

Ince Blundell has other structures of interest to the folly hunter. In front of the house is a Monument - a white Tuscan column with one eagle - and at the southern end of the park there is a magnificent Lion Gate standing alongside the main road. Also alongside the main road is the Priest's House opposite the Victorian estate entrance. This is a circular building, with a circular chimney and flattened sides.

Attached to the hall is the Holy Family Church. A unique night-time ceremony is held here each year, in which graves in the cemetery are decorated with flowers and candles prior to a candlelit procession and church service. This custom is traditional in Belgium and was reputedly introduced to Ince Blundell at the turn of this century.

Knowsley Hall - between Liverpool and St Helens. Map ref: SJ 45 94 Landranger 108.

Knowsley Hall has a number of buildings of interest to the folly hunter. First there is a square tower at the side of White Man's Dam. (The White Man is actually a lead statue on a pedestal.) Also there is the Octagon, a summer house dating from 1755, intended as an eyecatcher, east of the house. The interior is stucco decorated.

Lancaster - The Music Room. Map ref: SD 47 61 Landranger 97.

This lovely little building was built in 1730 for Dr Marton, Vicar of Lancaster, as a summerhouse or pavilion in what was once a private garden. The garden, however, disappeared with the construction of Sun Street, and the building became hemmed in by houses and sheds. This three-storeyed building is essentially a baroque façade with a central Ionic triumphal arch at ground floor level. The interior contains fine baroque plasterwork which has recently been restored by the Landmark Trust, who also removed some of the encroaching buildings. Depicted on the walls are the Muses of History, Music, Astronomy, Tragedy, Eloquence, Rhetoric, Comedy, Dancing and Amorous Poetry. It has been suggested that the name "Music Room" is perhaps a corruption of "Muses Room", the name referring to the plasterwork.

Liverpool - Sefton Park. Map ref: SJ 375 875 Landranger 108.

Sefton Park contains a number of buildings and monuments of interest to folly hunters. There is a lake with a series of small pools leading to a grotto, north of which stands a replica of Alfred Gilbert's Shaftesbury Memorial (better known as Eros in Piccadilly Circus). There is also a copy of the Peter Pan Statue (1928) the original of which stands in Kensington Gardens. Seek out also two Lodges and an excellent Palm House dating from 1896. It contains a number of statues. In the park you will also find the Samuel Smith Obelisk, which carries bronze reliefs.

Liverpool -   Wavertree. Map ref: SJ 387 893 Landranger 108.
On the green in Wavertree village is a curious octagonal Lock-up with a pointed roof which dates from 1796.

Manchester -   Heaton Park. Map ref: SD 839 045 Landranger
                    109

Heaton Park, with its Hall, lake, golf courses, woodlands and vast open spaces is Manchester's playground. It originally was the home of Sir Thomas Egerton, the first earl of Wilton. It also contains a number of interesting follies.

Smithy Lodge, by the eastern entrance, is an octagonal building with eight tuscan columns. It was designed by Lewis Wyatt and built in 1806.

To the North East of the Hall there is a Temple on the hill, boarded up and vandalised, a small rotunda of Tuscan columns with a dome and lantern. The Temple was reputedly built as an observatory, for it is reported that the first earl bought a telescope

from Dollonds in 1803 for £18 5s 0d.

The Papal Monument, a shapeless block of granite in the southwestern corner of the park, looking for all the world like some bizarre glacial erratic, commemorates the visit of Pope John Paul II to Manchester in 1982. It is erected on the spot from which he conducted a mass attended by over 30,000 people.

Temple, Heaton Park

The Manchester Town Hall Portico, Heaton Park

The Telecommunications Tower on the northern side of the park stands at the highest point in Manchester. It is 230 feet high and bristles with dishes and aerials. It is run by British Telecom and forms part of the national radio relay system for the trunk telephone and television network.

The Manchester Town Hall Portico, Manchester's "Great Gate of Kiev", which stands by the lake, is Heaton Park's finest (and most obvious) folly. The town hall it came from originally stood in King Street, Manchester. It was designed by Francis Goodwin and was constructed 1819-34. The portico was rebuilt here in 1912, about the same time as the construction of the lake, to which it makes an excellent foil. Four enormous Ionic columns support the architrave between its two end bays, which contain niches with statues.

Milnthorpe - St Anthony's Tower. Map ref: SD 499 822
Landranger 97.

Milnthorpe is not (and never has been) in Lancashire, but its location by Morecambe Bay, lying between Silverdale and Grange, makes it worthy of mention. The round, grey tower, standing on the hilltop behind Milnthorpe, and offering fine views over the Kent Sands is not served by any public right of way. The tower contains a vaulted ground floor chamber, and a first floor room reached by

St Anthony's Tower, Milnthorpe

a winding external stair (now locked). From there an internal stair once wound up to the roof of the tower, where the stump of a flagpole is still visible.

The tower was built by Henry Smithies to commemorate the passing of the 1832 Reform Bill (an excuse for folly builders all over the country - see the Parbold Bottle). Wainwright states that it was built as a summerhouse for nearby St Anthony's House, which stands down on the main road. Yet this building speaks for itself, having nothing of the summerhouse about it. With its steps and martial appearance, it is very much a prospect tower. (Although of course it could have served both functions.) In World War II it was used as an observation post, being manned by the Home Guard. Today it stands ruinous and derelict.

Ormskirk - Parish Church. Map ref: SD 413 085 Landranger 108.

The Parish Church of St Peter and St Paul, Ormskirk, is unusual in that it possesses both a steeple and a tower. It is locally known as the "Sisters Folly". According to legend, two sisters who endowed money to the church could not agree on whether the church should have a steeple or a tower, so in the end they built both. The story is almost certainly apocryphal, for the steeple is the older of the two, dating from the fifteenth century. It has been twice rebuilt, which tends to make it look more modern than the tower. The battlemented tower was built in the sixteenth century using masonry plundered from Burscough Priory. It was built to accommodate the bells from the priory, which were brought to Ormskirk after the Dissolution.

Ormskirk itself also has a Clock Tower at the junction of Church Street. This was erected by public subscription in 1896 on the site of the old market cross.

Prestwich - Philips Park. Map ref: SD 797 041 Landranger 109. Worthy of a visit if you have exhausted the facilities of nearby Heaton Park. Not easy to find. The Italianate villa of the Philips family was demolished in 1950. Philips & Co were Manchester merchants. Mark Philips was one of the first MPs for Manchester after the passing of the Reform Bill. The follies here consist of a

conservatory and a temple. The conservatory is ruinous, but is currently being restored, the temple (when you find it) is a bit of a disappointment. Pleasant walks, though, with lots of dense woodland, scrub, and even a lake. An unexpectedly peaceful and sylvan landscape is hidden here, secluded, surrounded by industrial desolation and tucked neatly away beneath the busy M62.

Temple, Philips Park, Prestwich

Royton -   Tandle Hill Monument. Map ref: SD 901 089 Landranger 109.

At the north western corner of Tandle Hill country park. An obelisk.

Scarisbrick -   Scarisbrick Hall, Map ref: SD 392 126 Landranger 108, near Southport.

Scarisbrick Hall is not a folly, but as one of the craziest, most eccentric structures in the whole of Lancashire it most certainly deserves a mention in this book. Only Conishead Priory at Ulverston comes anywhere near it for high Victorian bad taste. The hall was designed by Augustus Welby Pugin in 1840 and completed in 1868 by Pugin's son, Edward. Pugin the Elder was responsible (an apt word!) for designing the House of Commons, and one look at Scarisbrick instantly betrays the connection. The house was commissioned by Charles Scarisbrick, High Sheriff of Lancashire, who was a bachelor, recluse and noted eccentric. When Scarisbrick died suddenly in 1860, his will required his undertakers to carry his coffin in a straight line from Scarisbrick Hall to Bescar Chapel, where a gap had been ready made in the presbytery garden wall. Consequently the funeral procession had to cross potato fields, pass through gaps cut in hedgerows and cross planks laid over ditches!

Charles' equally eccentric sister Anne inherited the house on her brother's death and set out to finish where he had left off. The original clock tower had been designed as a runner-up for Big Ben, but Lady Anne instead commissioned an incredibly disproportionate Gothic tower over 100 feet high, which looks poised to pull the house over onto its side. On the flat coastal plain, it makes a landmark which can be seen for miles. When Lady Anne invited Gladstone to visit just before Christmas 1867, she illuminated the whole neighbourhood with lights, and bathed her fantastically ornate home in a multicoloured glow, while her servants let off flares and fireworks from the rooftops. Today this magnificent neo-Gothic masterpiece is a private boarding school for boys.

Silverdale -   Lindeth Tower. Map Ref: SD 461 742 Landranger 97.

Located near Gibraltar Farm alongside the lane leading down from Silverdale to Jenny Brown's Point. Lindeth Tower (now known as Tower House) stands securely hidden behind its high wall and "private" notices. The upper part is visible from the roadside. This tall, grey castellated tower was erected as a belvedere in 1842 by Henry Paul Fleetwood, who owned the adjacent house and was related to Sir Peter Hesketh Fleetwood of Rossall Hall, the man largely responsible for the town that now bears his name.

The tower is best known for its literary associations, for it was for some years after 1850 regularly occupied by the novelist and biographer of Charlotte Brontë, Mrs Elizabeth Cleghorn Gaskell. Mrs Gaskell came to Silverdale during the summer months to escape the smoke and smog of Manchester where she lived. Here at this peaceful spot, with its woods, crags, salt marshes and endless sands, she walked, relaxed and worked on novels later to become famous. Of her novels, *Cranford*, which is supposedly based on Knutsford in Cheshire, is in fact the old-fashioned name for nearby Carnforth; and Silverdale itself was described in her novel *Ruth* under the name of Abermouth.

Sunderland Point - Sambo's Grave. Map ref: SD 422 561
Landranger 102.

Sambo's Grave is not a folly, but it most certainly is a curiosity, and as such deserves a mention in this book. Situated at the Mouth of the Lune, frequently cut off by the tide, Sunderland Point is a slumbering land that time has forgotten. Once Lancaster's chief port, it was eclipsed in the eighteenth century. Now Sunderland Point is left alone with its memories. A footpath, running over sandy soil between brambles, gorse and wild flowers, leads to the seaward side of the point, a realm of salt marshes and shimmering haze.

A left turn leads to Sambo's Grave, a stone slab set into a little grassy plot between a fence and a wall. Yet this is not what attracts the eye - rather it is the touching little wooden cross and the jamjar urn filled with wild flowers. Sambo was an African slave who arrived here in 1736, no doubt as a household servant accompanying his master, possibly a sea captain. It is said he died of a broken heart when his master left him. Being a "black heathen", the local churchgoers refused him a plot in their graveyard, so he was buried here at this remote and secluded spot. It seems to me that the heathen got the better deal - for while their forgotten graves crumble Sambo's is tenderly maintained. An old brass tablet touchingly tells all in the form of a uniquely lyrical epitaph:

Here lies   Poor SAMBOO
                A Faithfull NEGRO
                       Who
    (Attending his Maſter from the Weſt Indies)
       DIED on his arrival at SUNDERLAND

Full sixty Years the angry Winter's Wave
Has thundering dashd this bleak & barren Shore
Since SAMBO's Head laid in this lonely GRAVE,
Lies still & ne'er will hear their turmoil more.
Full many a Sandbird chirps upon the Sod
And many a Moonlight Elfin round him trips
Full many a Summer's Sunbeam warms the Clod
And many a teeming Cloud upon him drips
But still he sleeps - till the awakening Sounds
Of the Archangel's Trump new Life impart
Then the GREAT JUDGE his APPROBATION founds
Not on Man's COLOR but his WORTH of HEART.
James Watson Scr.   H.Bell del.

                                    1796.

A smaller plaque, with an interesting motif above it, tells a sad story of vandalism and entreats us to

"RESPECT THIS LONELY GRAVE".

Uppermill - Pots and Pans. Map ref: SE 011 052 Landranger 109.

On the moors near Uppermill, this obelisk is set in a spectacular rocky location in the midst of superb south Pennine moorlands. It is however, a war memorial, so consequently has not been included in my catalogue of walks. Well worth a visit, if only for the fine upland ramble.

Walkden - Ellesmere Memorial. Map ref: SD 739 031 Landranger 109.

By the church in the centre of Walkden on the site of the original Bridgewater Offices and Sunday School. Built in the style of an Eleanor Cross the memorial is a tabernacle with a very high pinnacle, 50 feet high. It was erected in memory of Harriet, the wife of Francis Egerton, 1st Earl of Ellesmere, a much-loved lady who was a founder of local schools and a friend to the poor. On the corners figures (now missing) depicted a collier, a cotton worker and two factory girls. The larger statues, which still remain, are of chastity, prudence, piety and munificence. The monument was dedicated on 26th July 1869. Presiding over the ceremony was Mr Fereday Smith, who was also much involved with the construction of the other Ellesmere Memorial at nearby Worsley. The Memorial was originally surrounded with steps and railings but these have since disappeared.

Wigan - Tyldesley Memorial. Map ref: SD 585 065 Landranger 108.

Located alongside the busy A49 just north of Wigan town centre heading towards the infirmary, this square stone pillar with a ball finial must surely be one of the oldest war memorials in Britain, commemorating as it does events of the Civil War. Wigan was a Royalist town which saw much trouble during the Civil Wars. In 1651, after the execution of Charles I, the Prince of Wales (the future Charles II), was supported by the Earl of Derby, who had come out of exile, and northern Royalists rallied to him, including Sir Thomas Tyldesley of Myerscough Lodge, who had fought with him on many a campaign. On 25th August 1651 they were riding down

Wigan Lane when they were ambushed by a party of Roundheads. The earl had two horses shot from under him, but managed to make good his escape. Tyldesley, however, was less fortunate and was killed along with many others on this very spot.

A slate tablet affixed to one side of the monument tells the story of Sir Thomas's career. A second, more recent, tablet informs us that the memorial was restored by Wigan Corporation in 1886. Seeing the monument as it is now, standing in a flowerbed alongside a busy trunk road and surrounded by suburban housing, it is difficult to imagine the desperate events that must have taken place here all those centuries ago.

BIBLIOGRAPHY

Abercrombie, E. *Grange and the Cartmel Fells* Dalesman 1960

Abram, W.A. *History of Blackburn* 1877

Aspland, Lindsey *A Guide to Grange-over-Sands* Simpkin, Marshall

Baddeley, M.J.B. *The English Lake District. Thorough Guide* Ward Lock 1978

Barber, Henry *Furness and Cartmel Notes* Atkinson, Ulverston 1894

Battrick, Elizabeth *Guardian of the Lakes - A History of the National Trust in the Lake District from 1946* Westmorland Gazette 1987

Bingham, Roger K. *The Chronicles of Milnthorpe* Cicerone Press 1987

Birkett, H.F. *The Story of Ulverston* Titus Wilson 1949

Blackpool Tower 'The Tops' Souvenir Brochure 1988. First Leisure Plc.

Buck, G.R. *Walking in the Lancashire Pennines* Dalesman 1982

Burton, Anthony *The Shell Book of Curious Britain* David & Charles 1982

"Capernwray", *Lancashire Life* March 1983

"Clougha Pike and Windy Clough" supplement to *Lancaster Guardian* 6th July 1895

"Cumbria" *Grange and Cartmel A Practical Guide for Visitors* Dalesman 1976

Curwen, J. *Castles and Towers of Cumberland , Westmorland and Lancs North of the Sands* Titus Wilson, Kendal 1913

Darwen Advertiser. Article "India Mill" 14th December 1978

Darwen News 1932. Various correspondences and articles concerning Hollinshead Hall and its Wellhouse

Duckworth, Alan 1979 *A History of Darwen Tower 1898-1979* Darwen Libraries

Ekwall, Eilert, *The Place-Names of Lancashire* Manchester U.P., 1922

"Ellesmere Memorial Competition", *The Builder* 24th July 1858

"Ellesmere Memorial", *The Builder* 6th November 1858

Evans, A.L. *Lost Lancashire* Cicerone Press 1991

Eyre, Kathleen *Lancashire Landmarks* Dalesman 1976

Eyre, Kathleen *The Real Lancashire* Dalesman 1983

Goldthorpe, Ian *Rossendale Rambles* Rossendale Groundwork Trust 1985

Grange and District Natural History Society *Hampsfell Nature Trail* (leaflet)

Grange Guide Book 1973

Headley, G. & Meulenkamp, W. *Follies - A National Trust Guide* Jonathan Cape 1986

Holland, Eric "Opening the Hoad Monument", *The News* 24th April 1970

Houghton, George "Capernwray", *Lancaster Guardian* 29th June 1973

"Jubilee Tower", *Lancaster Guardian* 15th July 1977

"Jubilee Tower", *Lancaster Guardian* 12th October 1979

Lofthouse, J. *Lancashire's Fair Face* Hale 1976

Lord Peter & Susan *Rambling around Rossendale* Countryside Publications 1985

Macrory, Richard *Trans Pennine Walk - A 54 Mile Route from W Lancashire to Haworth* Dalesman 1983

Mee, Arthur *The Kings England - Lancashire* Hodder & Stoughton. Revised A.F.Kersting 1973

Millward, Roy *Lancashire* Hodder & Stoughton 1955

North Lonsdale Magazine, Vol.1

North West Civic Trust - *The Treasures of Lancashire* NWCT 1989

"Old Worsley, Some Historical Notes", *The Journal* 17th March 1933

The Lake District Ordnance Survey Landranger Guidebook, Jarrold 1988

Pape, T. "Grange and Some of its Lovely Surroundings" *Morecambe "Visitor"* 30th August 1911

Peter, David *In and Around Silverdale* Lunesdale Publishing, Carnforth 1984

Pevsner, Nikolaus *The Buildings of England. S. Lancashire* Penguin 1969

Pownall, David *Twixt Ribble & Lune* Victor Gollancz 1980

Raistrick, Arthur *Industrial Archaeology* Paladin 1972

Sephton John *A Handbook of Lancashire Place Names* Liverpool, Young 1913

Sewart, Alan & Dorothy *Lancashire Leisure Guide* Robert Hale 1989

Spartina *Looking at South Lancashire* Dalesman 1971

Twycross, E. *Mansions of England & Wales - County Palatine of Lancaster* 1846

Twycross, *Mansions of England and Wales* Vol. II

Wainwright, A. *A Furness Sketchbook* Westmorland Gazette 1978

Wainwright, A. *Westmorland Heritage* Westmorland Gazette 1975

Welsh, Frank, *The Companion Guide to the Lake District* Collins 1989

Whitaker, Terence W. *North Country Ghosts & Legends* Grafton Books 1988

CICERONE GUIDES

Cicerone publish a wide range of reliable guides to walking and climbing abroad

FRANCE
TOUR OF MONT BLANC
CHAMONIX MONT BLANC - A Walking Guide
TOUR OF THE OISANS: GR54
WALKING THE FRENCH ALPS: GR5
THE CORSICAN HIGH LEVEL ROUTE: GR20
THE WAY OF ST JAMES: GR65
THE PYRENEAN TRAIL: GR10
THE RLS (Stevenson) TRAIL
TOUR OF THE QUEYRAS
ROCK CLIMBS IN THE VERDON
WALKS IN VOLCANO COUNTRY (Auvergne)
WALKING THE FRENCH GORGES (Provence)
FRENCH ROCK

FRANCE / SPAIN
WALKS AND CLIMBS IN THE PYRENEES
ROCK CLIMBS IN THE PYRENEES

SPAIN
WALKS & CLIMBS IN THE PICOS DE EUROPA
WALKING IN MALLORCA
BIRDWATCHING IN MALLORCA
COSTA BLANCA CLIMBS
ANDALUSIAN ROCK CLIMBS
THE WAY OF ST JAMES

FRANCE / SWITZERLAND
THE JURA - Walking the High Route and
    Winter Ski Traverses
CHAMONIX TO ZERMATT The Walker's
    Haute Route

SWITZERLAND
WALKING IN THE BERNESE ALPS
CENTRAL SWITZERLAND
WALKS IN THE ENGADINE
WALKING IN TICINO
THE VALAIS - A Walking Guide
THE ALPINE PASS ROUTE

GERMANY / AUSTRIA / EASTERN EUROPE
THE KALKALPEN TRAVERSE
KLETTERSTEIG - Scrambles
WALKING IN THE BLACK FOREST
MOUNTAIN WALKING IN AUSTRIA
WALKING IN THE HARZ MOUNTAINS
WALKING IN THE SALZKAMMERGUT
KING LUDWIG WAY
HUT-TO-HUT IN THE STUBAI ALPS
THE HIGH TATRAS

ITALY & SLOVENIA
ALTA VIA - High Level Walkis in the Dolomites
VIA FERRATA - Scrambles in the Dolomites
ITALIAN ROCK - Rock Climbs in Northern Italy
CLASSIC CLIMBS IN THE DOLOMITES
WALKING IN THE DOLOMITES
THE JULIAN ALPS

MEDITERRANEAN COUNTRIES
THE MOUNTAINS OF GREECE
CRETE: Off the beaten track
TREKS & CLIMBS IN WADI RUM, JORDAN
THE ATLAS MOUNTAINS
WALKS & CLIMBS IN THE ALA DAG (Turkey)

OTHER COUNTRIES
ADVENTURE TREKS - W. N. AMERICA
ADVENTURE TREKS - NEPAL
ANNAPURNA TREKKERS GUIDE
CLASSIC TRAMPS IN NEW ZEALAND
TREKKING IN THE CAUCAUSUS

GENERAL OUTDOOR BOOKS
THE HILL WALKERS MANUAL
FIRST AID FOR HILLWALKERS
MOUNTAIN WEATHER
MOUNTAINEERING LITERATURE
THE ADVENTURE ALTERNATIVE
MODERN ALPINE CLIMBING
ROPE TECHNIQUES IN MOUNTAINEERING
MODERN SNOW & ICE TECHNIQUES
LIMESTONE -100 BEST CLIMBS IN BRITAIN

CANOEING
SNOWDONIA WILD WATER, SEA & SURF
WILDWATER CANOEING
CANOEIST'S GUIDE TO THE NORTH EAST

CARTOON BOOKS
ON FOOT & FINGER
ON MORE FEET & FINGERS
LAUGHS ALONG THE PENNINE WAY

*Also a full range of guidebooks
to walking, scrambling, ice-climbing,
rock climbing, and other adventurous
pursuits in Britain and abroad*

*Other guides are constantly being added to the Cicerone List.
Available from bookshops, outdoor equipment shops or direct (send for price list)
from CICERONE, 2 POLICE SQUARE, MILNTHORPE, CUMBRIA, LA7 7PY*

CICERONE GUIDES

Cicerone publish a wide range of reliable guides to walking and climbing in Britain, and other general interest books.

LAKE DISTRICT - General Books
A DREAM OF EDEN
LAKELAND VILLAGES
LAKELAND TOWNS
REFLECTIONS ON THE LAKES
OUR CUMBRIA
THE HIGH FELLS OF LAKELAND
CONISTON COPPER A History
LAKELAND - A taste to remember (Recipes)
THE LOST RESORT? (Morecambe)
CHRONICLES OF MILNTHORPE
LOST LANCASHIRE (Furness area)
THE PRIORY OF CARTMEL

LAKE DISTRICT - Guide Books
CASTLES IN CUMBRIA
THE CUMBRIA CYCLE WAY
WESTMORLAND HERITAGE WALK
IN SEARCH OF WESTMORLAND
CONISTON COPPER MINES Field Guide
SCRAMBLES IN THE LAKE DISTRICT
MORE SCRAMBLES IN THE LAKE DISTRICT
SHORT WALKS - SOUTH LAKELAND
WINTER CLIMBS IN THE LAKE DISTRICT
WALKS IN SILVERDALE/ARNSIDE
BIRDS OF MORECAMBE BAY
THE EDEN WAY
WALKING ROUND THE LAKES

NORTHERN ENGLAND (outside the Lakes
BIRDWATCHING ON MERSEYSIDE
CANAL WALKS Vol 1 North
CANOEISTS GUIDE TO THE NORTH EAST
THE CLEVELAND WAY & MISSING LINK
THE DALES WAY
DOUGLAS VALLEY WAY
HADRIANS WALL Vol 1 The Wall Walk
HERITAGE TRAILS IN NW ENGLAND
THE ISLE OF MAN COASTAL PATH
IVORY TOWERS & DRESSED STONES (Follies)
THE LANCASTER CANAL
LANCASTER CANAL WALKS
LAUGHS ALONG THE PENNINE WAY
A NORTHERN COAST-TO-COAST
NORTH YORK MOORS Walks
THE REIVERS WAY (Northumberland)
THE RIBBLE WAY
ROCK CLIMBS LANCASHIRE & NW
THE YORKSHIRE DALES A walker's guide
WALKING IN THE SOUTH PENNINES
WALKING IN THE NORTH PENNINES
WALKS IN THE YORKSHIRE DALES (3 VOL)
WALKS IN LANCASHIRE WITCH COUNTRY
WALKS IN THE NORTH YORK MOORS
WALKS TO YORKSHIRE WATERFALLS (2 vol)
WALKS ON THE WEST PENNINE MOORS
WALKING NORTHERN RAILWAYS (2 vol)
WALKING IN THE WOLDS

DERBYSHIRE & EAST MIDLANDS
WHITE PEAK WALKS - 2 Vols
HIGH PEAK WALKS
WHITE PEAK WAY
KINDER LOG
THE VIKING WAY
THE DEVIL'S MILL / WHISTLING CLOUGH (Novels)

WALES & WEST MIDLANDS
THE RIDGES OF SNOWDONIA
HILLWALKING IN SNOWDONIA
HILL WALKING IN WALES (2 Vols)
ASCENT OF SNOWDON
WELSH WINTER CLIMBS
SNOWDONIA WHITE WATER SEA & SURF
SCRAMBLES IN SNOWDONIA
SARN HELEN Walking Roman Road
ROCK CLIMBS IN WEST MIDLANDS
THE SHROPSHIRE HILLS A Walker's Guide
HEREFORD & THE WYE VALLEY A Walker's Guide
THE WYE VALLEY WALK

SOUTH & SOUTH WEST ENGLAND
COTSWOLD WAY
EXMOOR & THE QUANTOCKS
THE KENNET & AVON WALK
THE SOUTHERN-COAST-TO-COAST
SOUTH DOWNS WAY & DOWNS LINK
SOUTH WEST WAY - 2 Vol
WALKING IN THE CHILTERNS
WALKING ON DARTMOOR
WALKERS GUIDE TO DARTMOOR PUBS
WALKS IN KENT
THE WEALDWAY & VANGUARD WAY

SCOTLAND
THE BORDER COUNTRY - WALKERS GUIDE
SCRAMBLES IN LOCHABER
SCRAMBLES IN SKYE
THE ISLAND OF RHUM
CAIRNGORMS WINTER CLIMBS
THE CAIRNGORM GLENS (Mountainbike Guide)
THE ATHOLL GLENS (Mountainbike Guide)
WINTER CLIMBS BEN NEVIS & GLENCOE
SCOTTISH RAILWAY WALKS
TORRIDON A Walker's Guide
SKI TOURING IN SCOTLAND

REGIONAL BOOKS UK & IRELAND
THE MOUNTAINS OF ENGLAND & WALES
    VOL 1 WALES VOL 2 ENGLAND
THE MOUNTAINS OF IRELAND
THE ALTERNATIVE PENNINE WAY
THE PACKHORSE BRIDGES OF ENGLAND
THE RELATIVE HILLS OF BRITAIN
LIMESTONE - 100 BEST CLIMBS

*Also a full range of EUROPEAN and OVERSEAS
guidebooks - walking, long distance trails,
scrambling, ice-climbing, rock climbing.*

*Other guides are constantly being added to the Cicerone List.
Available from bookshops, outdoor equipment shops or direct (send s.a.e. for price list) from
CICERONE, 2 POLICE SQUARE, MILNTHORPE, CUMBRIA, LA7 7PY*

Printed by CARNMOR PRINT & DESIGN
95-97 LONDON ROAD, PRESTON, LANCASHIRE, UK.